Yes! You can create... a Sindy Doll sized M_____ ___om

Rawles

1:6 scale
Fashion Doll size

With easy step by step instructions for beginners.

Yes! You can create a Sindy Doll sized messy bedroom

By
Deborah Rawles

The name "Sindy" is used with kind permission from
Jerry Reynolds – CEO Pedigree Group Ltd

With thanks to:

God
Mum
Isabella

Imagine your dolls having so many accessories that they do not know where to put them. What's more, imagine that you are the one able to create them! It is fun to see what other skilled crafters can make. Wonderful to see all the new things they have made for their own dolls. Inspiring to gaze at the rooms and scenes they have created.

In this book "Yes! You can create a Sindy Doll sized messy bedroom", you will follow very simple step by step instructions so you can create these items for yourself. You can learn the easy to follow skills to craft an endless supply of jewellery and accessories, just for your own dolls.

Each "make" has been designed to be easy for you to complete successfully. Made with inexpensive things you may already have around the house.

Let's start with something that is super easy.

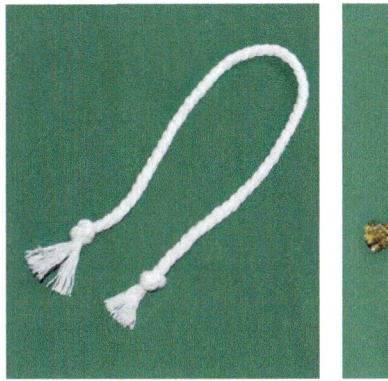

Rope and Ribbon Belts

You will need:

- Any spare lengths of ribbon or stringing.
- PVA white craft glue (not essential)
- Scissors
- Ruler

Method:

Tie a knot in the end of your chosen ribbon or rope, as close to the end as you can.

Measure 16cm or 6 inches along from the knot and tie another knot at that point. It may take some time to get it in the right place, don't rush it and tighten it too quickly. Only pull it tight when you are happy with the position.

Cut the ribbon about 1cm or ¼ inch after the second knot you have tied.

To stop the ribbon or rope from fraying (coming unraveled) put a little bit of white glue on each end and allow it to dry completely.

When the glue has dried completely, you can tie it around the waist of your doll.

They also make great hair ties.

With endless colours and patterns of ribbon, you can quickly make a wide selection of belts for your dolls.

Easy Bead Necklaces

You will need:

- Small beads
- Stringing thread
- Glue
- Scissors

Method:

This is another quick way to create a huge variety of designs relatively quickly. Thread the beads on to the stringing thread while the thread is still on the reel. If you intend to be careful with your necklaces then sewing thread is fine. Do not cut the thread to length and then try to thread the beads on as they do love to drop off the other end and it is harder to tie it off when you have finished.

Thread enough beads on to the thread so that it fits over your dolls head.

Tie off the ends when you are happy with it and add a small dot of glue to the knot to stop it coming undone.

More advanced necklace method:

To make the flower pattern with the seed beads, as shown in the first picture, you will need 2 colours of beads.
112 darker colour and 32 lighter.

They will be used in a repeat pattern 4 times.
28 x 4 darker beads.
8 x 4 lighter beads.

It may look complicated but, as you will see, it is easy.

Thread 14 darker beads on to your stringing thread.

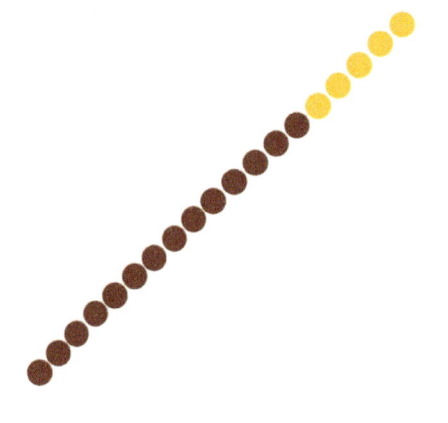

Next 5 lighter beads.

Then 1 darker bead.

This is where the clever bit starts.

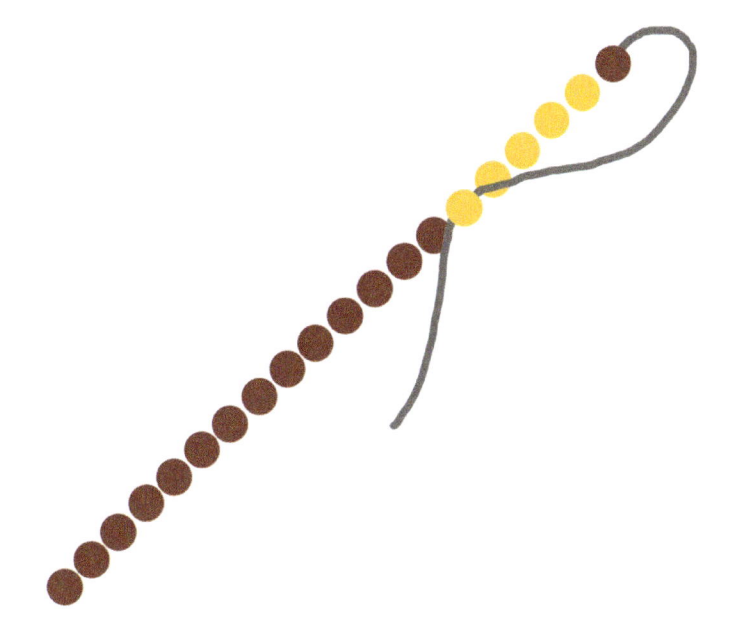

Make sure you have plenty of spare thread ahead of the beads you have just put on and take the end of the thread. Thread it back through the hole of the very first lighter bead you put on first.

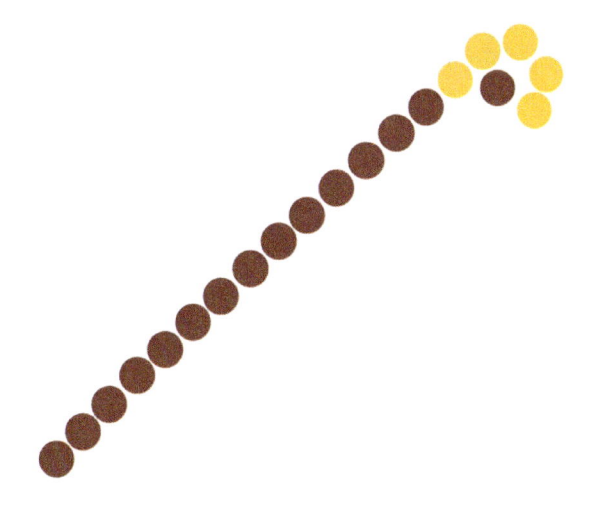

Pull it so the beads gather up, you will see it has formed half of a flower.

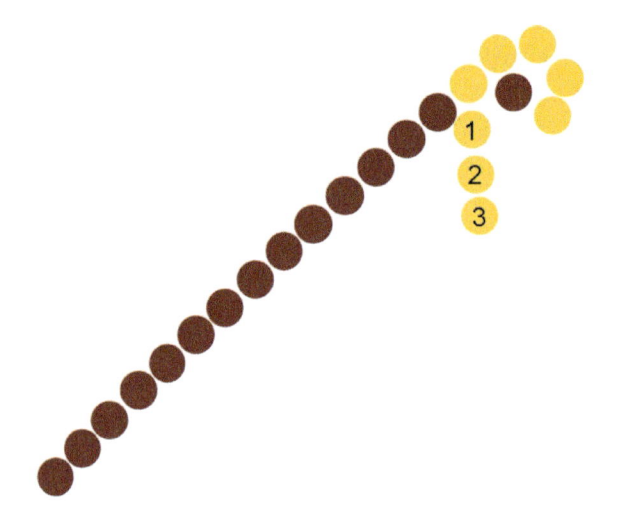

Next add 3 more lighter coloured beads.

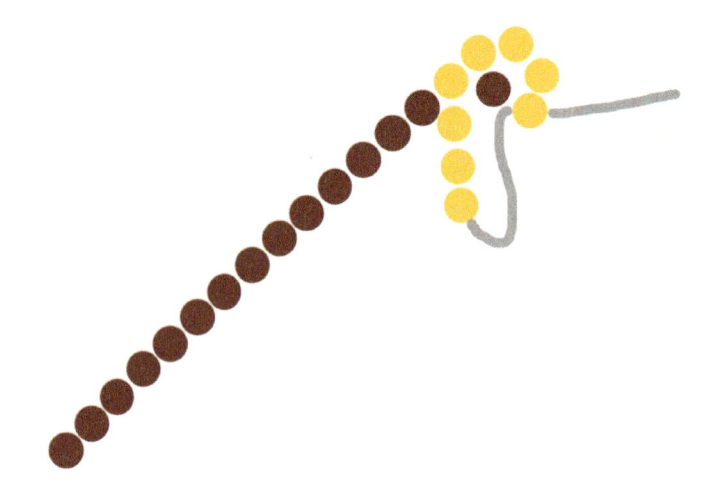

Thread back up through the fifth lighter bead you put on.

Add 14 more of the darker beads to complete the pattern.

Repeat this 4 times and tie off your necklace.

You can make lots of different designs just by changing the types of beads.

You could use a mix of colours, it is entirely up to you.

These necklaces are made from Hama, Perler or Pyssla plastic beads. They are inexpensive and the colours are bright.

You might even have a small bead bracelet that you could make shorter for your dolls.

Choker Necklaces

You will need:

- Metal paperclips or the metal wire edge of a spiral bound note pad (some are coated in plastic)
- Beads with holes big enough to fit on the wire
- Two pairs of pliers
- A Ruler

Method:

Straighten out your choice of wire and cut to a length of 6 ½ cm or 2 5/8 inches.

Bend over 8mm or 5/16ths inch at one end at a right angle.

If you have any round nosed pliers bend it over and your loop is done.
Regular pliers read on.

Bend a third of that at an opposite right angle.

Bend two thirds down over to create a hook.

Continue to bend the end with your pliers until it creates a loop.

Thread your chosen beads on to the other end of the wire. The loop you just made will stop them from dropping off.

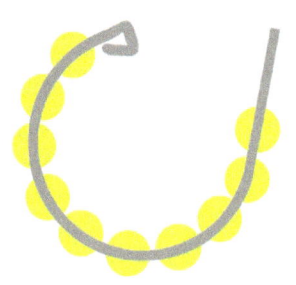

Bend the wire into a circle shape.

Create a loop exactly as you did earlier. Make sure you have bent the beaded wire in to a circle before you create the loop, as the beads take up more space on the wire as you curve it round.

Your Choker Necklace is complete! Again you can use any choice of beads. Make sure not to leave any clothes or metal on your doll for a long time. Remove everything for storage as a doll's skin can become coloured by anything against it for a very long time.

If you make the wire length shorter, you can make a matching bracelet. This is made from Sterling Silver Wire and Crystals.

Advanced Level Necklace and Earrings

You will need:

For the necklace
- 17 seed beads
- 6 tube beads
- Bead stringing wire or thread
- 2 crimps
- 2 silver knot covers
- 1 small silver jump ring
- 1 long silver headpin
- Pliers
- Scissors

For the earrings

- 4 seed beads
- 4 tube beads
- 6 silver headpins
- 4 silver jump rings

Method:

To make the necklace.

Cut a 15cm or 6 inch length of Stringing wire thread.

Fold over the wire and slot on a crimp bead.

As close to the end of the folded wire as you can, squeeze it flat using the pliers.

Cut off the extra piece of wire thread.

Thread the other end of the stringing wire into the hole at the bottom of one of the knot covers. The crimp stops the thread from coming out of the Knot cover.

Close up the Knot cover so it hides the end of the wire thread and crimp bead. Once you have mastered this technique, you can make lots of doll necklaces that fasten at the back of the neck.

Take the Long Headpin and snip off the lump.

Using pliers bend it into a spiral and create a loop as you did for the ends of the choker necklace.

Before closing the loop, hook on the small silver Jump Ring. Then close the loop so it cannot come off.

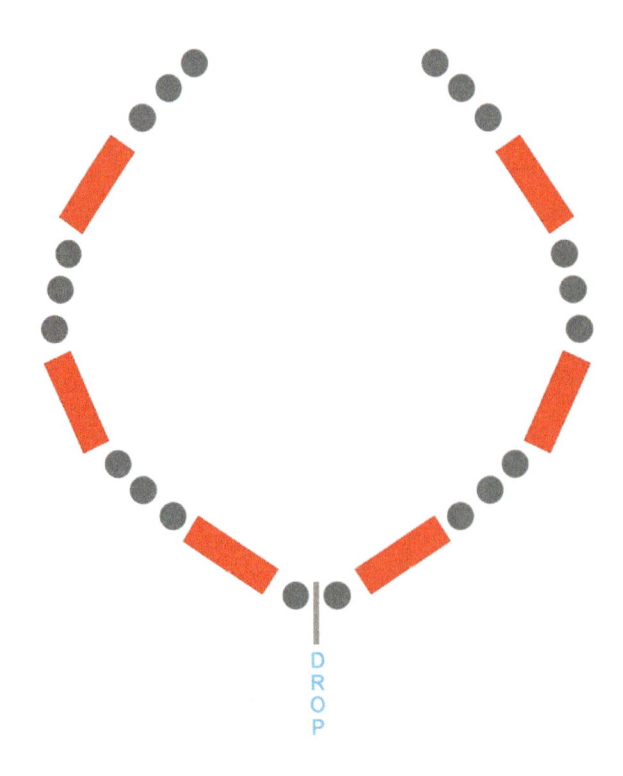

DROP

Thread your beads as follows:

3 Seed Beads
1 Tube Bead
3 Seed Beads
1 Tube Bead
3 Seed Beads
1 Tube Bead
1 Seed Bead

Add your Jump Ring that is now joined to the swirl pendant.

Complete the other half of the beading, reversing what you did before.

1 Seed Bead
1 Tube Bead
3 Seed Beads
1 Tube Bead
3 Seed Beads
1 Tube Bead
3 Seed Beads

Place on the Clam Shell.

Fold the Stringing wire thread as close as you can to the Clam Shell and squash the Crimp on to the fold so it cannot come off.

Cut off the extra Stringing Wire Thread and close up the Clam Shell.

Leave one Clam Shell hook open and close the other one, using Pliers, to create a loop.

<u>To make the Earrings</u>. These are suitable only for dolls with pierced ears.

Thread 1 Seed Bead and 1 Tube Bead on to each of the 4 Head Pins.

Cut them off so you have about 8mm or 5/16ths inch remaining and create a loop to make your drops.

Using Pliers open up one of the Jump rings and hook another on to it plus one end of one of the drop's loops you have just made. Do this again with another Jump ring.

Cut the lumps off of the remaining two Head pins.

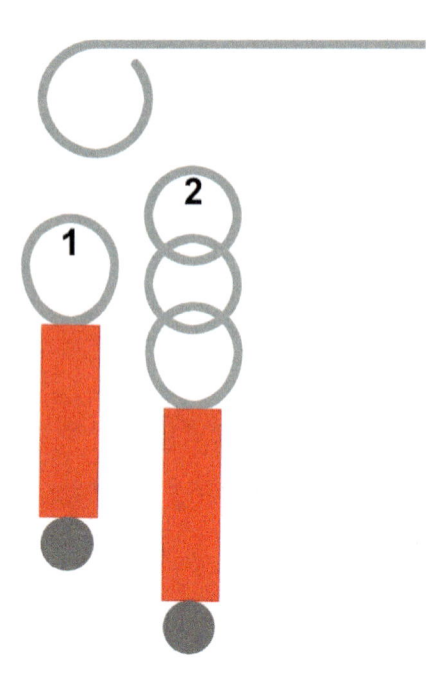

Create one loop at the end of each but before closing it up, hook on a beaded drop without the Jump rings and then one of the drops with the Jump rings on, as shown, on to the last jump ring not the drop itself.

Repeat this with the other Head pin and drops.

Cut the long length of headpin down, if needed, so they stay in your dolls ears.

Chain Necklace

You will need:

- 6 gold colour headpins
- A length of gold colour chain
- 1 gold colour bolt ring
- 6 seed beads
- 3 crystal beads
- Pliers
- Ruler

Method:

This necklace repeats a lot of the skills you have learned when making the previous necklaces. It looks more complicated because of the chain but it is straight forward.

You will need to open the links of the chain using pliers so you have 3 lengths.
2 lengths with three links and 1 length measuring about 7cm or 2 ½ inches.

Take a headpin and thread 1 seed bead, 1 crystal bead and 1 seed bead on to it.

Cut it off allowing enough to create a loop just as you did before.

Before closing the loop, thread a link on to the end of the shortest chains you made. This will be your first earring drop.

Make another earring drop to match the first.

Make another drop but this time without the chain. This will be your necklace pendant.

Take 2 headpins and cut off the lumps.

Create a loop at the end of them and, before closing the loop, hook on the other ends of the shortest chain links on the earring drops.

To make the necklace, open the bolt ring and hook it on to the end of the longest chain you made and close the bolt ring.

Thread the pendant you made on to the chain.

Take the last Headpin and cut off the lump.

Create a loop at one end but leave it open.

Bend the Headpin into the shape show, and before closing the loop, hook on the other end of the chain.

Close the loop to complete your necklace.

By changing the colours and the arrangements of the beads, you can make very different sets of jewellery for your dolls, to match any outfit.

Triple Strand Pearl Necklace

If you have completed the previous jewellery makes, you are now ready for this one.

You will need:

- Pearl Seed Beads
- 2 gold colour clam shells
- 2 crimps
- Pliers
- Bead stringing thread
- Ruler
- Scissors

Method:

Thread enough seed beads on to the thread so that it fits around your dolls neck nicely.

Cut the thread so you have plenty at each end to work with.

Thread another length of beads but this time with 10 more beads than the first one.

Place this to one side.

Thread a third length of beads with 10 more than the second string (20 more than your first string).

Take one end of each and together thread the three strings into the clam shell, being careful not to lose the beads from the other ends.

Fold over the ends and flatten the crimp in place just like you did for the other jewellery set earlier.

Cut off the extra threads and close the Clam shell over the crimp.

Repeat this at the other end, making sure to allow enough thread so the beads can bend around the neck of your doll, and close the clam shell.

Leave one Clam shell as a hook and the other close the loop to create the fastening.

Perfume Bottles

You will need:

- Old beads in different sizes
- Head pins or regular pins that fit in the bead holes
- Glue
- Silver card
- Ruler
- Pencil
- Scissors
- Wire cutters
- Sandpaper or nail file

Method:

Take a small bead and thread it on to the pin.

Repeat with the various beads you have so that you have a large bead on the bottom. It can take a little while to get an arrangement that you are happy with. A small bead measuring about 5mm (3/16 inch), then a flat spacer bead followed by a large 1.5cm (1/2 inch) bead works well.

When you are happy with the arrangement, take the pin out and cut off the extra wire plus a little extra.

Put some glue on the pin and slide the beads back on to the pin, in the order you were happy with, to create your perfume bottles.

Allow the glue to dry completely.

Take the silver card and cut it to 4.5cm by 3cm (1 ¼ inch by 1 ¾ inch). This will be your mirrored bedside tray.

Take one of your perfume bottles and, holding it upright, drag the bottom of it along some sandpaper or a nail file until it has a flat bottom.
Repeat the bottom sanding with each of the bottles you have made.

Glue three perfume bottles at the back of the tray and one in front to complete this make.

Pompom Teddy Bear

You will need:
- Assorted size Pompoms
- Googly wiggle eyes
- Glue

Method:

Take two medium sized Pompoms and glue them together.

Take 6 Pompoms, about half the width of the first, and glue two to the head for ears and four to the body as arms and legs.

Take a different colour Pompom smaller than the rest and glue this to the middle of the head for a nose.

Choose two small Googly wiggle eyes and glue them in place.

By changing the colours and sizes of the Pompoms, you can make very different Teddy Bears.

Easy Felt Scarf

You will need:

- Felt fabric
- Scissors
- Ruler

Method:

Cut a strip of Felt fabric measuring 2.5cm (1 inch) wide by 23cm (9 inches) long.

Snip in at the ends in 2cm (3/4 inch) cuts to make the fringe.

Doll sized books

You will need:

- White card
- Ruler
- Scissors
- Pencil
- Glue
- Magazine pictures (or the page at the back of this book if you have bought a paper copy)
- A Craft knife

Method:

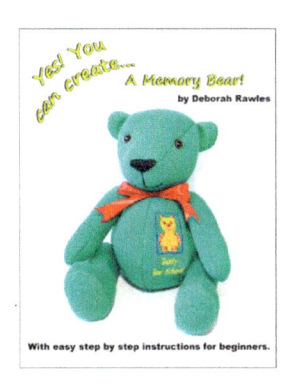

If you are using magazine pictures then the front cover should measure 3.2cm (1 ¼ inches) by 4.2cm (1 5/8 inches). You will need a picture for the front and back covers.

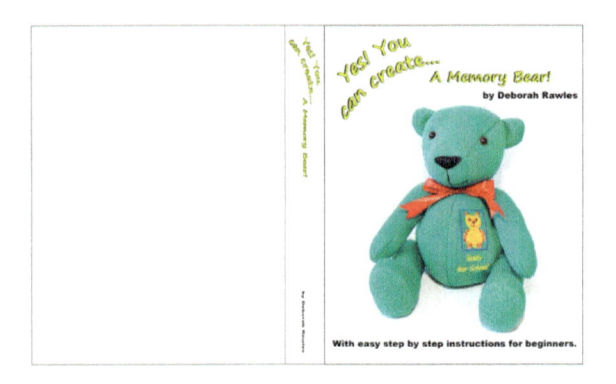

Glue these to a piece of White card with a 5mm (3/16 inch) gap between them for the spine of the book.

Cut out the whole piece.

If you are using the pictures at the back of the book cut them out and glue them to some White card.

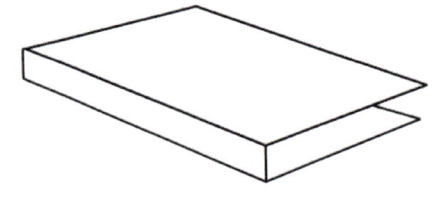

Score along either side of the spine with a craft knife and fold it over to make the book cover.

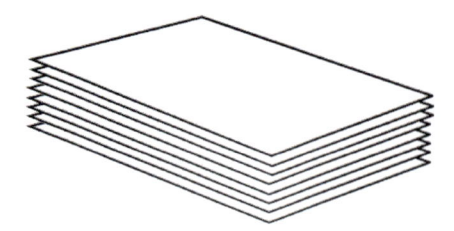

Measure the front of your book and cut out more pieces of White card slightly smaller than your measurement. You will need to make enough of these so that when you stack them neatly one on top of the other, they fill the inside of your book to make the pages.

Run some glue along the longer edges of your card stack and place them inside your book cover. Allow the glue to dry completely.

By varying the side of the book cover you can make all sorts of books.

You could use a different coloured card for the cover, and write on it, to make a gratitude journal.

Christmas or Birthday cards are also fun to remake into doll sized book covers.

Tiny wooden pencil

You will need:

- Wooden Cocktail Stick
- Ruler
- Craft Knife
- Black Felt Tipped Colouring Pen

Method:

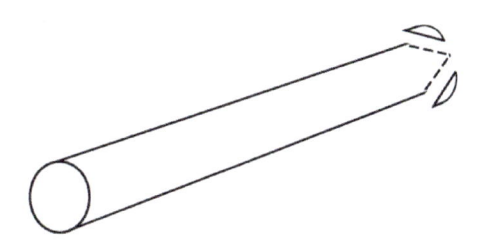

Carefully sharpen one end of the Cocktail Stick using the Craft Knife, making sure to move the knife away from yourself with each cut, and making sure your eyes are protected from any flying pieces.

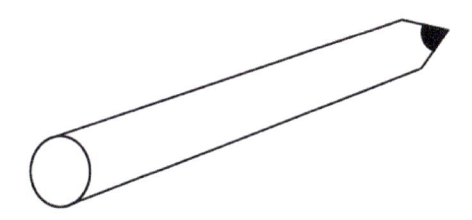

Cut the other end off in a straight cut and colour in just the point of your tiny pencil.

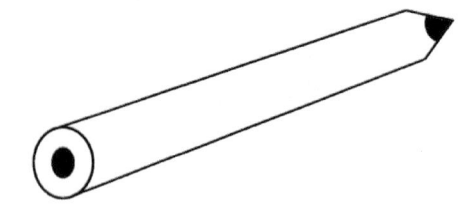

Draw a tiny dot on the other end in the middle.

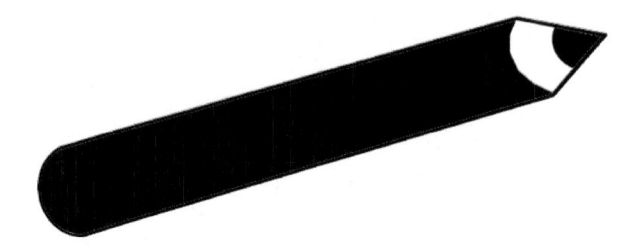

Colour in the outside of the pencil only to complete it.

By using different coloured felt pens you can make many art supplies for your doll.

Wall Calendar

You will need:
- White paper or Card
- Ruler
- Black Pen
- A picture

Method:

If you have bought a paper copy of this book, then you can just cut out the picture starring Comet the Dalmatian Molly and place it on your dolls wall.

If you are making your own then cut out your chosen picture or photograph and glue it to some paper or card allowing a gap underneath it for your calendar squares.

Divide and mark the squares 7 across and 5 down, using a pencil and pressing lightly in case of any errors.

When you are happy with the squares, draw them in Black pen.

Write tiny numbers at the top left of each square or just make a little squiggle to represent the numbers and write your chosen month at the top in larger writing.

Cut out your calendar page.

You could circle a special date in red pen, maybe your birthday!

Walls and Window

The walls are simply two pieces of Artists Acrylic Painting Boards 508mm by 406mm (20in by 16in), also known as Canvas Panels. You could cover strong cardboard box card in wallpaper samples or wrapping paper instead.
If you have a paper copy of this book please find the window picture at the back, cut it out, and your make is complete.

To make the Window.

You will need:

- A magazine picture or photograph of scenery or white paper, paint and a paint brush
- Thick white card
- Scissors
- Ruler
- Pencil
- Glue

If you have paper and paints, begin by mixing some blue paint with plenty of water and lightly wash the whole piece of white card.

Take a tissue or piece of kitchen roll and dab patches of the wet paint. The paint will lift to make clouds.

Allow it to dry completely before the next step.

Take some green paint and if it is a little light add a small amount of red to darken it.

With a dry brush put it in the paint and dot it on in an area at the bottom of the picture to make foliage.

Allow it to dry.

To make the window frame.

Measure the width of your magazine picture, photograph or painting and cut 3 strips of card this length.

Next measure the height and cut 3 strips of card this length.

Take one of each length and glue them across the centre of the picture in a cross.

Next cut the ends of the other pieces at a 45 degree angle, so the corners meet, and glue them all around the edges to complete the window frame.

Dolly Bed

You will need:

- An empty card breakfast cereal box big enough for your doll to lay on
- Fabric (an old T-shirt is great!)
- Sewing needle and Thread to match the fabric (or fabric glue)
- Scissors
- Glue
- Stuffing or cut up fabric scraps
- Old newspaper or packaging

Method:

Take your cereal box and open it along the side join, turn it inside out and glue it back together along the side seem.

Glue the bottom of the box together and when it has dried, stuff the box with old newspapers or packaging materials to make the bed more solid.

Glue some fabric over the top and sides of the box, folding the corners neatly and gluing them in place on the underside of the box.

Cut a piece of fabric that is wider than the box and sides added together and allow a bit extra for seems. If you use Cotton T-shirting then you do not need to sew seems but it does give a nice finish.

Fold over each edge at a time and sew a running stitch to tidy them up. You can add a length of old ribbon for decoration at this point. Alternately, fix the edges and ribbon with fabric glue.

To make the pillow, measure the width of your doll bed and cut two pieces of fabric that are this width and half the measurement for length.

Join the pillow pieces inside out by stitching or using fabric glue around the edges. Leave a gap for stuffing.

Turn the pillow in the right way and stuff it with batting stuffing or old scraps of fabric.

Sew up the gap to complete your doll bed.

Bedside Table

You will need:

- 2 Cereal boxes or light brown card
- A Ruler
- Pencil
- Scissors
- Glue
- 2 Beads
- Brown pencil
- A Craft knife

Method:

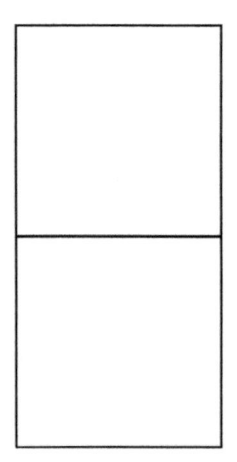

Open out the cereal box and draw to squares joined together measuring 9cm (3 ½ inches).

Draw a gluing flap at the end.

Cut out 2 of these.

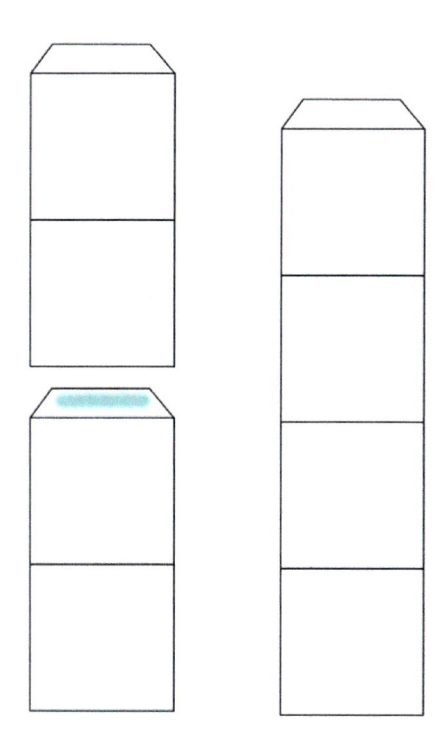

Glue one of the flaps and attach it to the straight edge of the other piece to make a run of 4 squares.

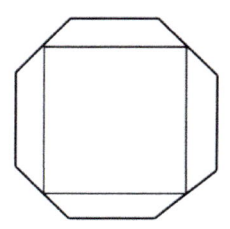

Draw another square with flaps on every edge.

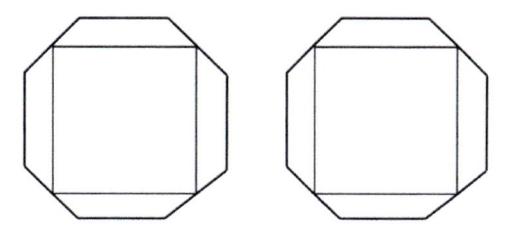

Cut out 2 of these.

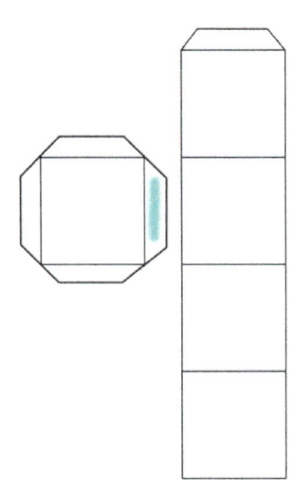

Glue one of these flaps two the second square in the run you just made.

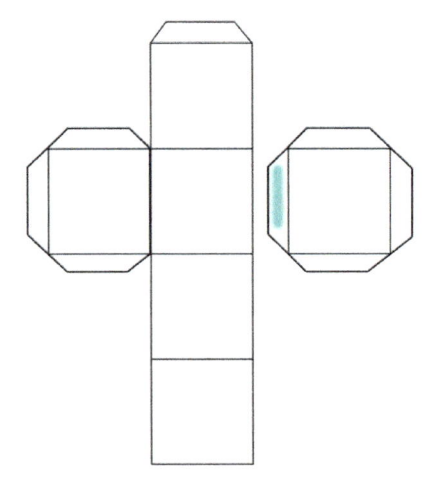

Glue the remaining square to the other side of the second square to create a cross shape. This is called a "Box Net" and is useful for making any box.

Score along the lines and fold up your box.

Add glue to the flaps and glue them to the edges they meet to create your bedside table.

Draw to horizontal lines to represent drawers in brown pencil and glue the beads on for handles and your bedside table is ready to display your dolly makes.

Wardrobe Unit

You will need:

- A cardboard box made from corrugated fiberboard cardboard

- Scissors
- A Craft knife
- Craft glue
- Ruler
- Bamboo skewer
- Pencil

Method:

Cut a piece of corrugated cardboard measuring 18cm by 30cm (7 inches by 12 inches). This is the back piece.

Cut 3 pieces measuring 9cm by 30cm (3.5 inches by 12 inches). These are the vertical pieces.

Cut 3 pieces measuring 7.5cm by 9cm (3 inches by 3.5 inches). These are the shelves.

Cut 2 pieces measuring 18cm by 9cm (7 inches by 3.5 inches). These are the top and bottom pieces.

Cut 4 small pieces measuring 2cm by 1.5cm (1 inch by ½ inch). These are the rail supports.

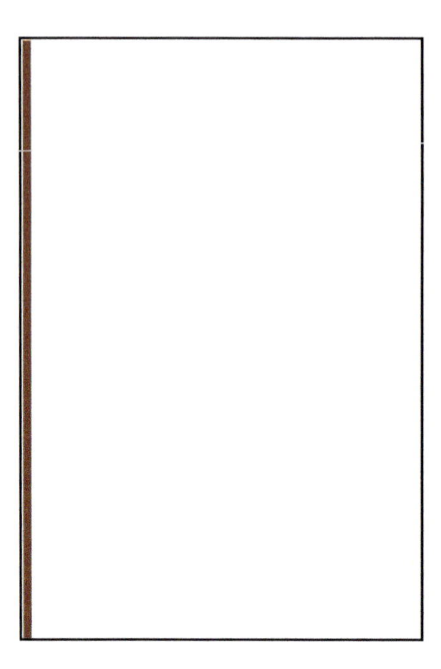

Take the largest piece and glue one of the longest vertical pieces on to it along the left hand side, as close to the edge as you can.

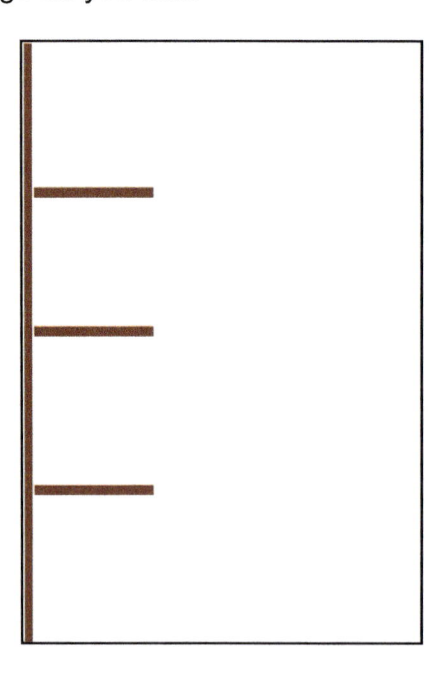

Next, take the 3 shelf pieces and glue them to the vertical piece you have just put on and the back piece.

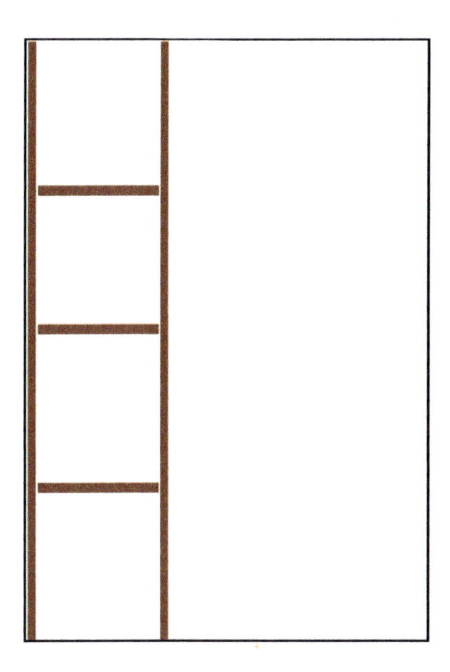

Next, take another longest vertical piece and glue it to the other side of the shelf pieces and back.

Take two of the smallest pieces and glue them together. Make a hole in the middle of them with your skewer. Do the same with the other 2 smallest pieces.

Glue one of these rail support pieces to the longest piece you have just glued on.

Glue the other to the other longest piece you have left over in the same position so the rail will be level when you put it in.

Hold this piece in place, but do not glue it yet, against the right hand side of the back piece and measure how long your rail needs to be.

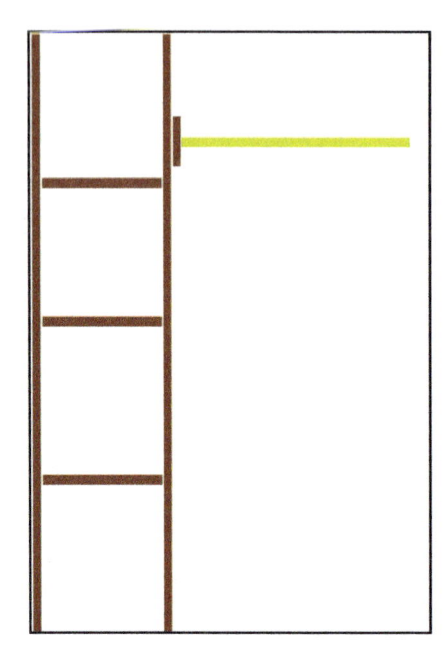

Cut your bamboo skewer to size and glue one end in to the rail holder you last glued on.

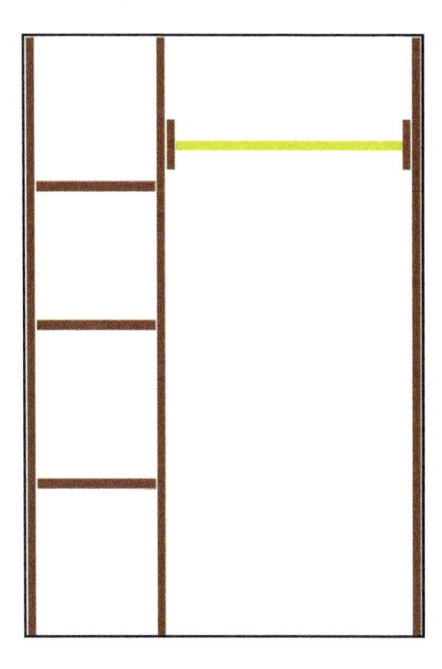

Put glue in the hole on the remaining longest piece and along the long edge and glue this in position, making sure to slot the rail in to the hole.

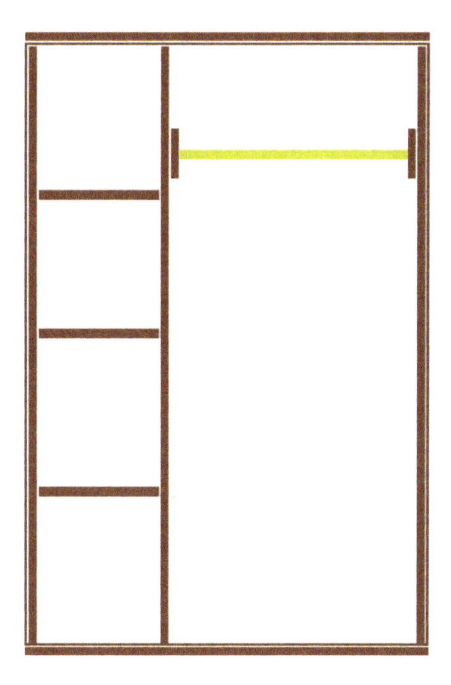

Glue the top and bottom pieces in place.

To neaten any corrugated edges, cut thin strips of card and peel off the flat card. Glue these over the edges to give the effect of laminated wood.

Coat Hangers

These are fun to make and use. Remember with storing clothes, it is best not to have anything next to them for a long time in case of reaction, these are just for play.

You will need:

- Wire
- Pliers
- Cutters
- Sandpaper or a nail file

Method:

File the end of your wire smooth, so there are no pointy edges.

Bend the end over by a small amount.

And squeeze it flat.

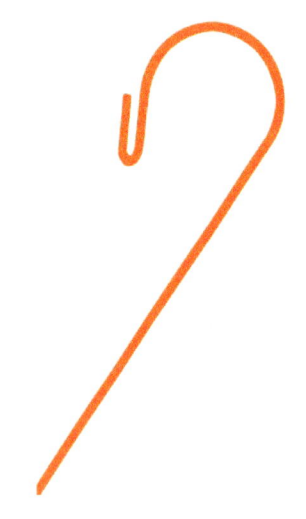

Create a curve, around a paintbrush may help.

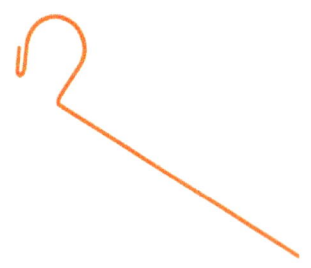

Next make a 45 degree corner bend.

Measure 3.5cm (1 ½ inches) and make a tighter bend in the opposite direction.

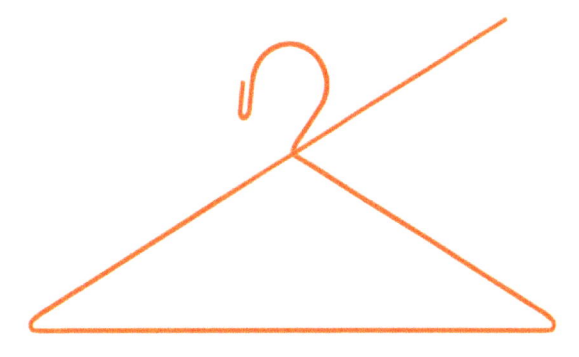

Measure 6.5cm (2 ½ inches) and make another tighter bend to mirror the one you just made. The wire should now be pointing at the corner bend. If not, just adjust your angle bends so it does.

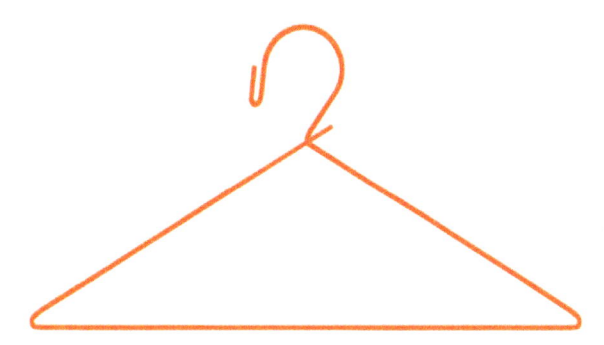

Allow a small amount of wire for finishing off your coat hanger and cut off the extra. File the edge smooth.

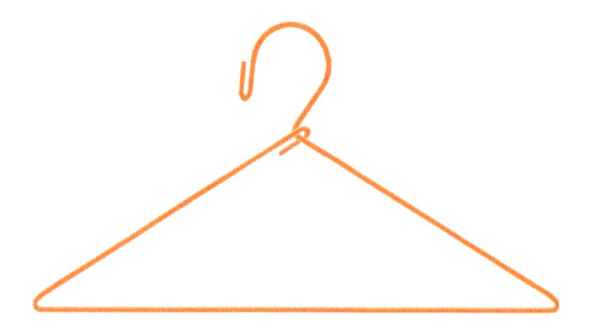

Finally bend the wire around the 45 degree corner bend so it holds in place and completes your coat hanger.

You can make several of these to hang in your wardrobe.

Shoe Boxes

You will need:

- Different coloured card
- Tissue
- Pencil
- Ruler
- Scissors
- Craft knife
- Glue

Method:

For the bottom of the Shoe Box cut a piece of card measuring exactly 6cm by 7.3cm (2 5/16th inch by 2 13/16th inch).

Draw a line 1.8cm (11/16th inch) in from the edge.

Do this for each edge and using a craft knife lightly score along the lines.

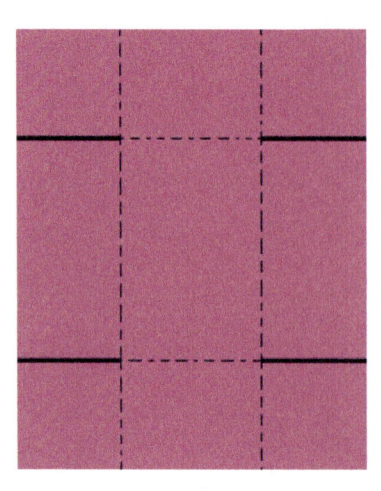

Using Scissors snip in at the sides, just along the solid lines shown, to create gluing flaps.

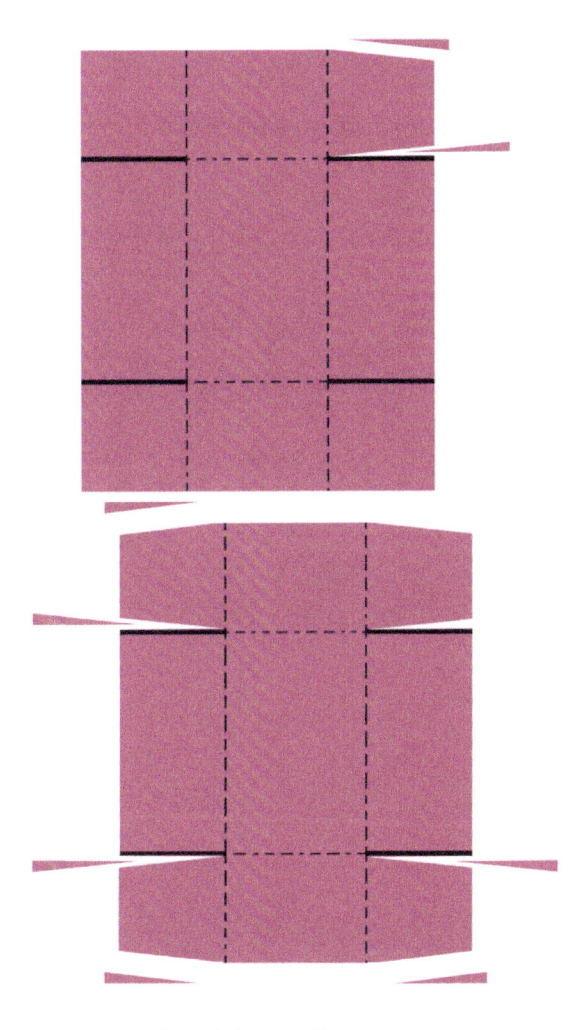

Snip off a small triangle off each side of these flaps.

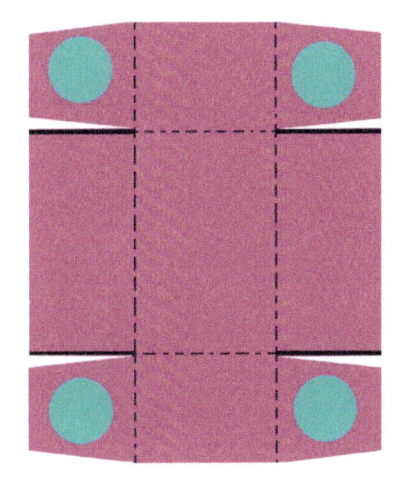

Fold up your Shoe Box bottom and place some glue on the glue flaps. Glue them inside the sides they meet.

The instructions are the same for the lid, just the card size changes.
Choose a contrasting colour card for the lid.

Cut a piece measuring exactly 3.8cm by 5.1cm (1 9/16th inch by 2 1/16th).

Draw lines 0.6cm (1/4 inch) in from the edges.

Repeat the above steps you used for the bottom of the box to finish off the lid.

Cut a piece of Tissue paper measuring 6cm by 8cm (2.5 inch by 3 inch). Scrunch it up and put it in the bottom of your Shoe Box and put on the lid.

You can make several Shoeboxes, in different coloured card, to place in the bottom of the Wardrobe.

Hat Box

This is made in the same way as the Shoeboxes except you start with a Hexagon. You will need to be able to use a protractor for this one or use the template at the back of this book.

You will need:

- A Protractor
- Different coloured card
- Pencil
- Ruler
- Scissors
- Craft knife
- Glue
- Paper

Method:

Draw a line in the middle of a piece of paper measuring 8cm (3 inches) and also mark the centre point at 4cm (1 ½ inches).

From the centre point mark the 60 degree point.

Mark the 120 degree point.

Repeat this on the other side of the line, marking both the 60 and 120 degree angles.

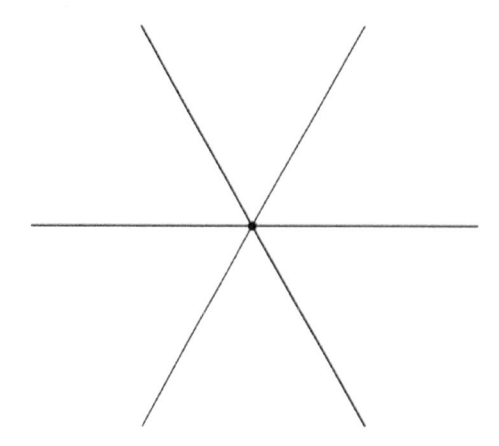

Join these lines, making sure the lines measure 8cm (3 inches), the centre point is at 4cm (1 ½ inches) and the line starts at 0.

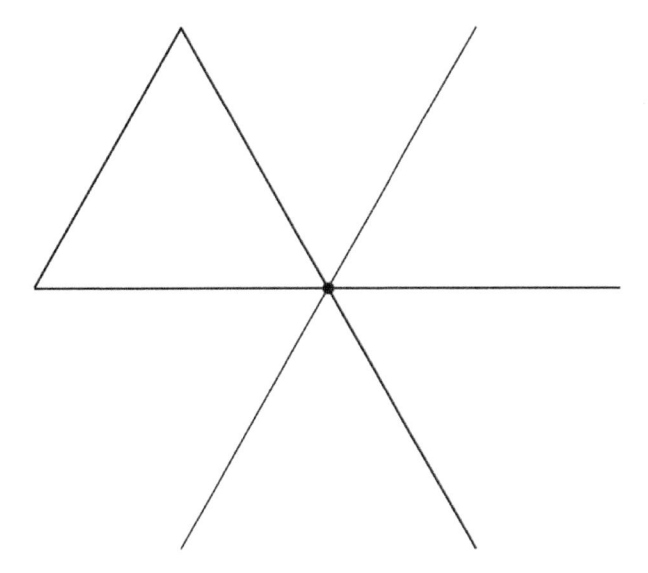

Join the ends of the lines together.

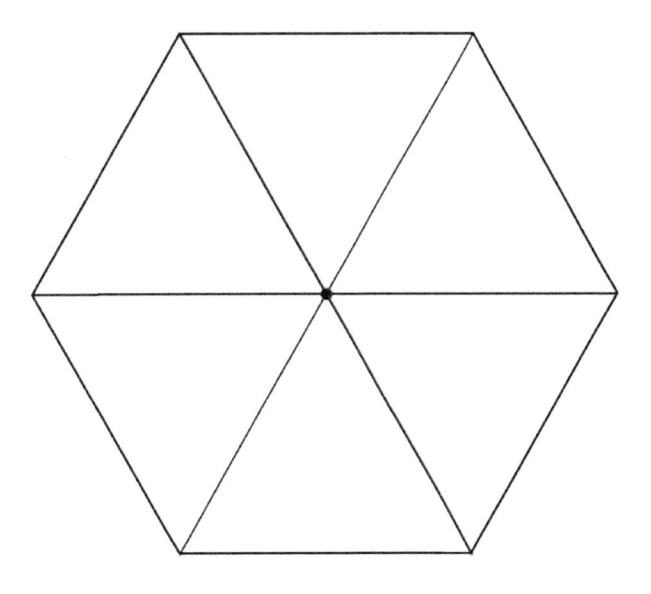

This will complete your hexagon shape. Cut it out.

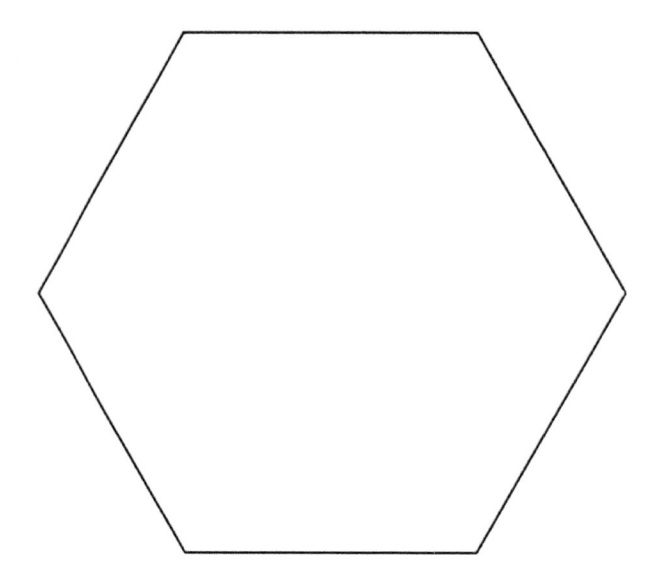

Draw around your hexagon template on to your choice of coloured card.

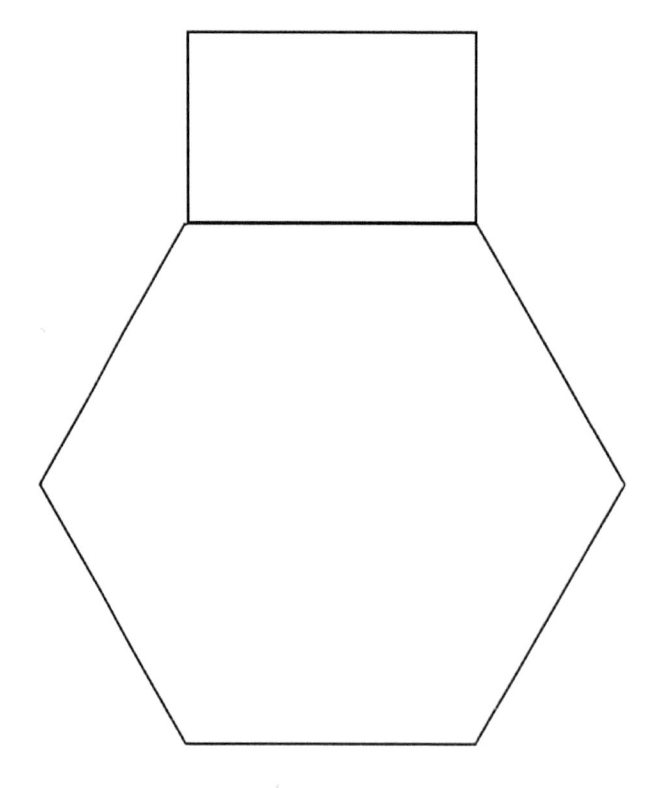

To make the sides of your Hatbox, draw a rectangle 2.5cm (1 inch) deep.

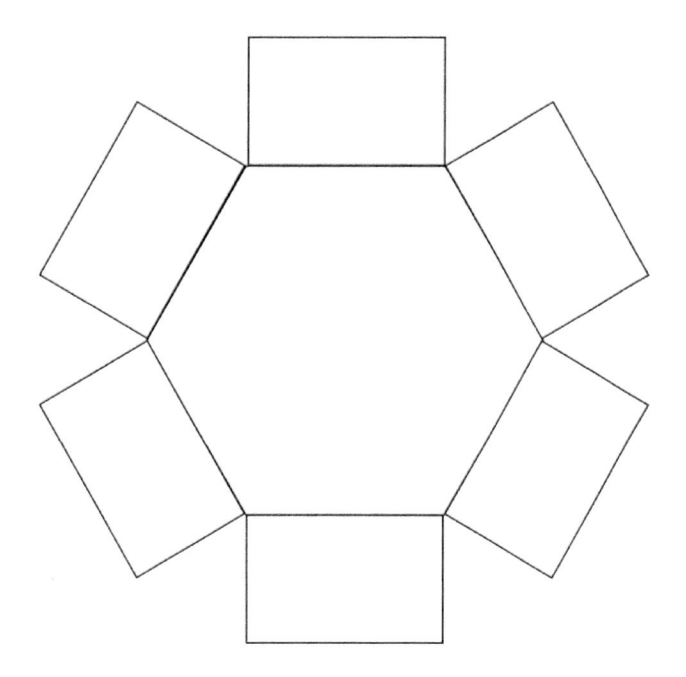

Do the same all the way around your hexagon's edges.

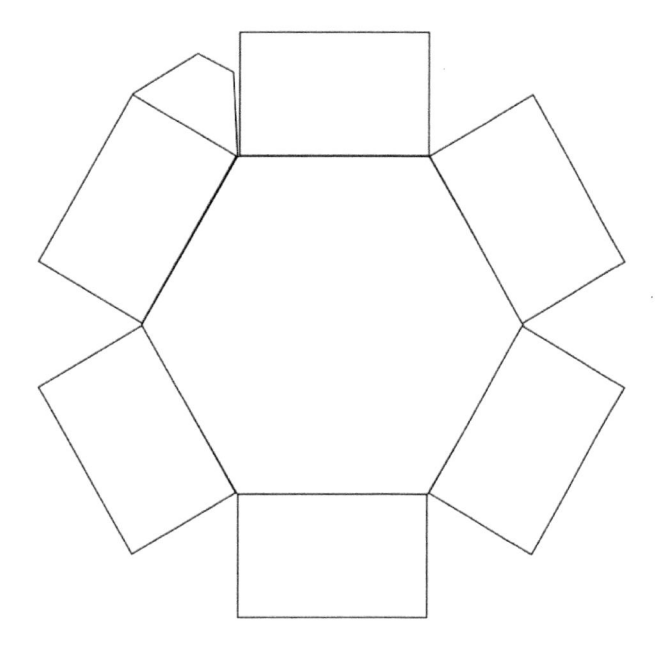

Draw a glue flap to one side of the rectangle.

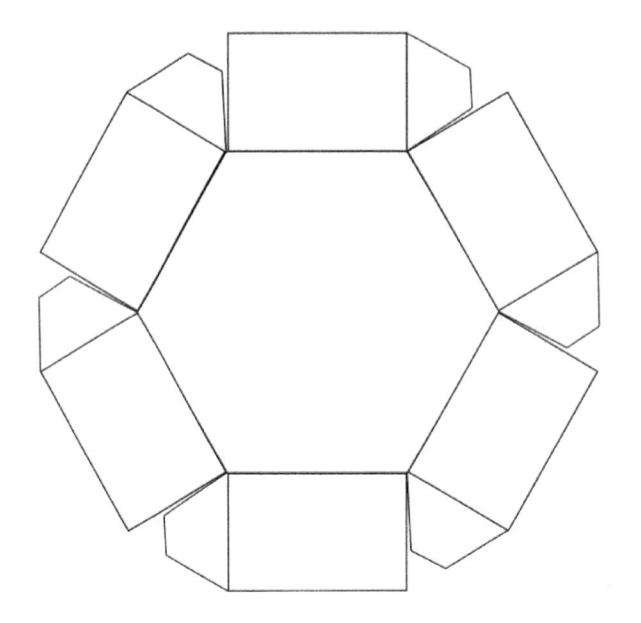

Draw a glue flap for every rectangle.

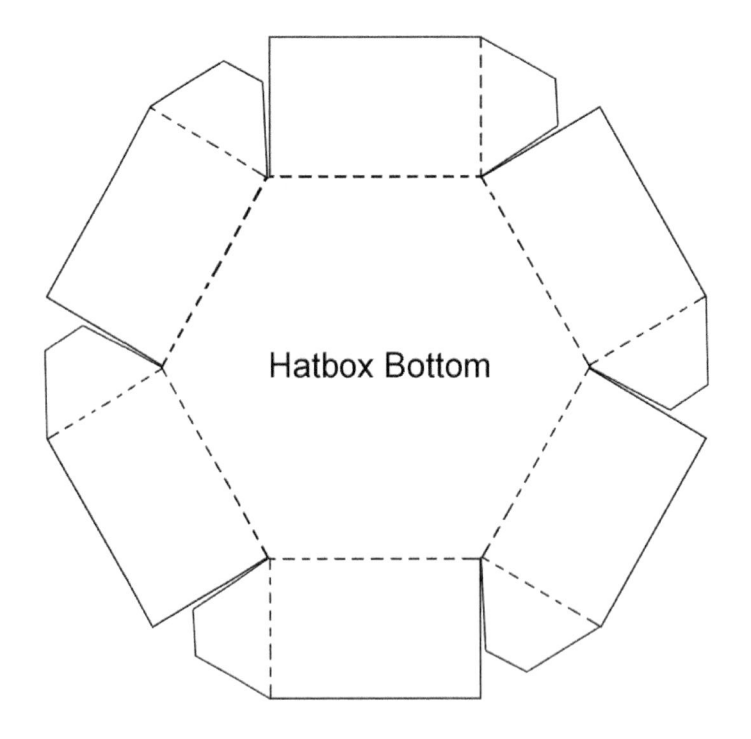

Hatbox Bottom

Score along the inside lines and cut it out.

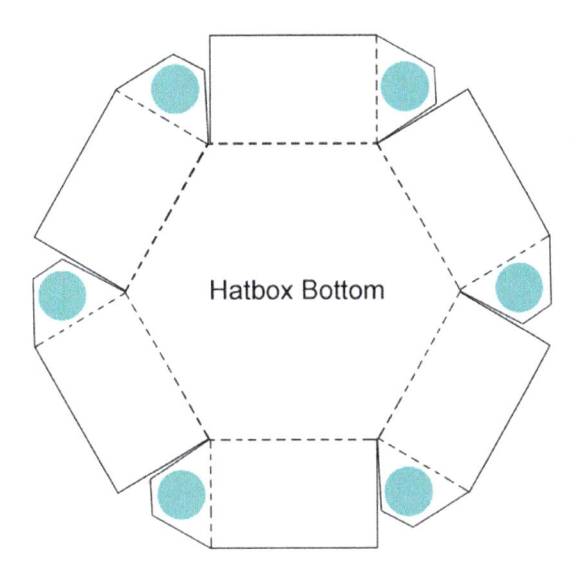

Fold up the Hatbox bottom and place glue on the glue flaps. Glue them to the sides they meet.

The lid is made in exactly the same way, except the hexagon is slightly bigger.

Using your original hexagon template, draw around it slightly larger. You only need it to be an extra 1mm (1/16th inch) all around.

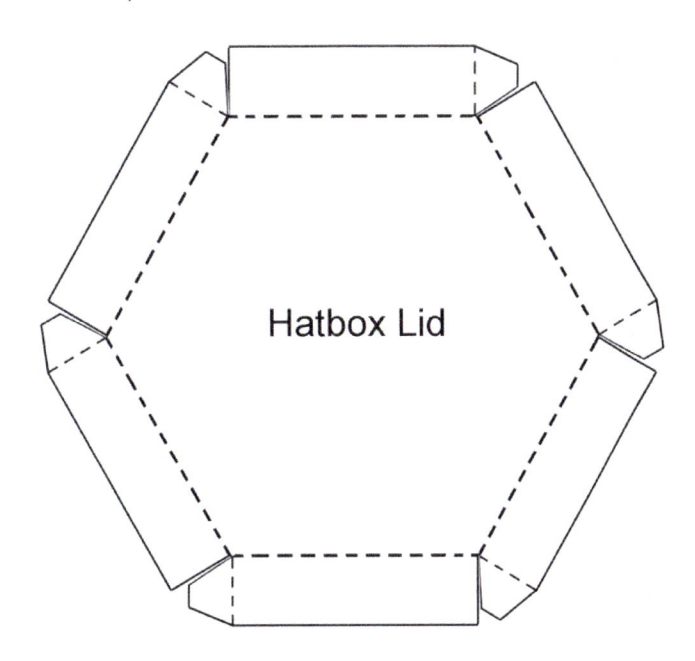

The side hexagons are 1cm (6/16th inch) deep.

Score along the dotted lines and cut out your Hatbox lid net.

Fold it up and place glue on the glue flaps.

Join these to the sides they meet.

When the glue has dried completely, place the lid on your Hatbox bottom and your Hatbox is complete.

Jewellery Box

This make uses an earring box with separate lid.
You may already have a hinged earring box you could use as a dolly jewellery box, without needing to hinge it.

You will need:

- An old earring box
- Coloured Felt
- Ribbon
- Glue
- Scissors
- Paper
- Pencil
- Sticky tape

Method:

Open your box and place the lid to one side. Remove the earring foam.

Draw around the base of your box or the foam piece, onto paper and cut it out slightly inside the lines.

Place the paper template inside the bottom of the box to check it fits.

Cut out a piece of Felt fabric using your paper template.

Glue the Felt piece in to the bottom of your box.

Sticky tape the lid to the base so that it will open and close nicely.

Glue one end of your ribbon to the bottom of the box at an angle pointing towards the lid.

Cut the ribbon to the correct length so it can be glued to the lid when it is open. The ribbon is there to stop the box lid from flopping off backwards when it is open.

Lay the box on its side and glue the top of the ribbon in position.

Fill your dolly Jewellery Box with the necklaces you made earlier.

Ribbon Belt

You will need:

- A length of ribbon
- 2 metal jump rings (approx 7mm or ¼ inch)
- PVA white glue or fabric glue
- Scissors
- Ruler

Method

Cut your Ribbon to 23cm (9 inches) long and put a little glue along the cut edge to stop the ends from fraying. Allow the glue to dry completely.

Thread the ribbon through the ribbon, fold the ribbon over by 1.5cm (1/4 inch), trapping the rings at the end of the fold, and glue the folded ribbon, with the rings in place.

When the glue has dried completely, your belt is complete. Now we may need to learn how to fasten it.

Wrap the belt around your doll so that the rings are at the front and thread the end of the ribbon through the loops.

You will see one loop is in front of the other.

Pass the end of the belt over this ring and back through the ring that is behind only.

Again, with a lot of these makes, by just changing the colour or pattern of the ribbon, you can make a huge selection of useful accessories for your doll.

Headscarf or Shawl

You will need:

- A piece of fabric measuring 17cm (7 inches) square
- Matching sewing thread and needle (or Fabric Glue)
- Scissors

Method:

Cut your square of fabric diagonally, from one corner to the other, to create two triangles.

Double fold one edge and sew it, or glue it, in place.

Do the same for the other edges to complete your Headscarf or Shawl.

If you use Cotton T-shirting fabric or Lycra / Spandex, then you do not have to sew or glue the edges.

By cutting a long strip of Lycra / Spandex, you can make hair ties for your doll to match it.

Legwarmers

You will need:

- Cotton T shirting material
- Matching sewing thread
- Needle
- Scissors

Method:

Cut two rectangles of Cotton T shirting measuring 6cm by 8.5cm (2 ½ inch by 3 inches).

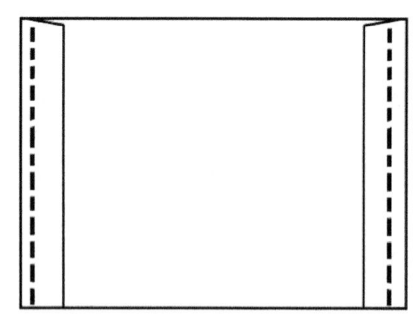

Fold over each 6cm (2 ½ inch) edge and sew a running stitch to secure in place.

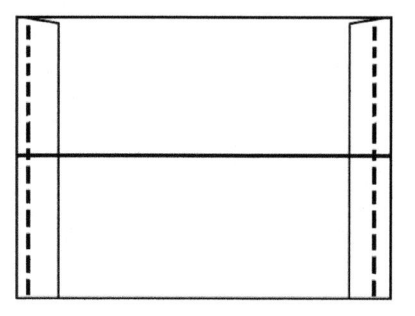

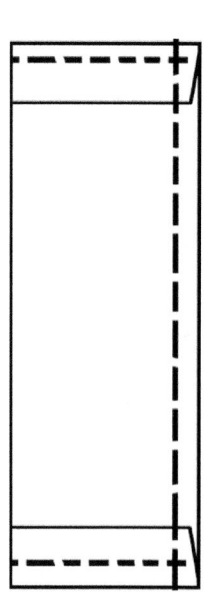

Fold them in half along the 6cm (2 ½ inch) edge, so that the folded edges are on the outside, and sew along the edge.

Turn them in the correct way to complete your legwarmers.

Sleeveless Short Dress

You will need to be able to sew a basic straight stitch and sew or hammer a popper/ snap fastener to complete this project.

You will need:

- Paper Pattern or 5mm squared paper (or Quad paper) and a Pencil
- Cotton Fabric (make sure this is colour safe)
- Matching sewing thread
- Needle
- Scissors
- Hammer Popper or Hammer Snap Fastener
- Hammer
- Ballpoint pen or fabric pen

Method:

If you have not bought the paper copy of this book then you will need to create your own paper pattern pieces.

Begin by copying the lines, square by square on to your own Squared paper.

Choose the smaller squared pieces if you are using the 5mm Squared Paper and the larger squares for Quad paper.

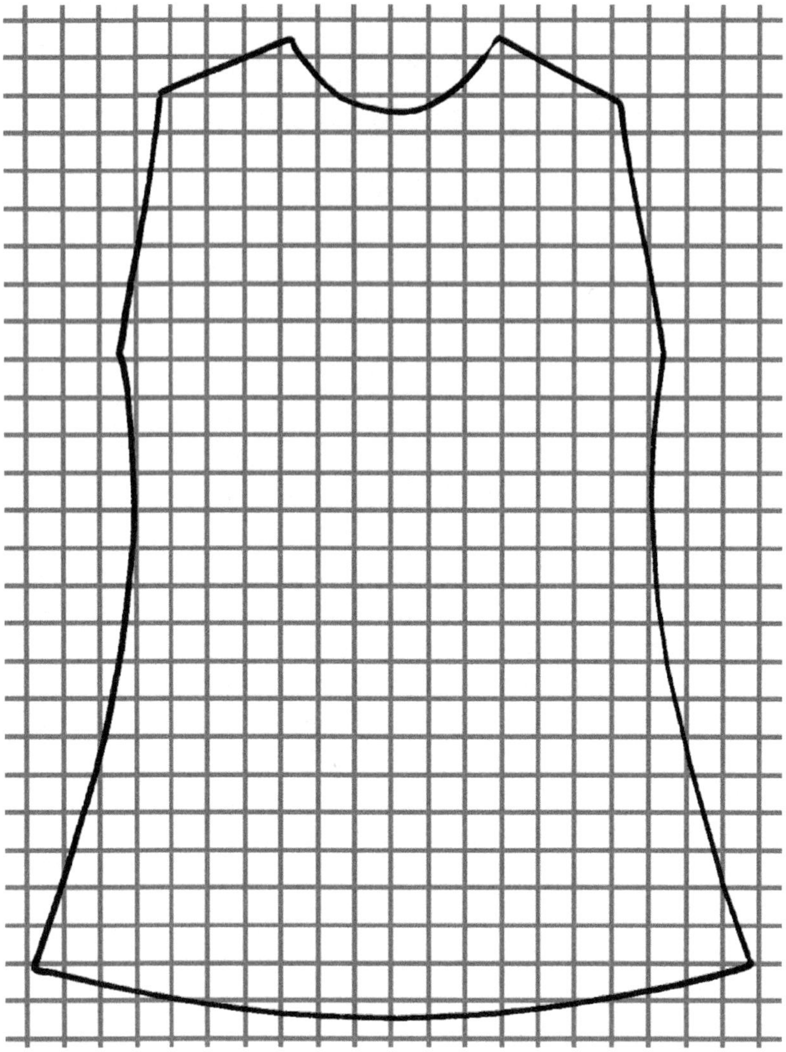

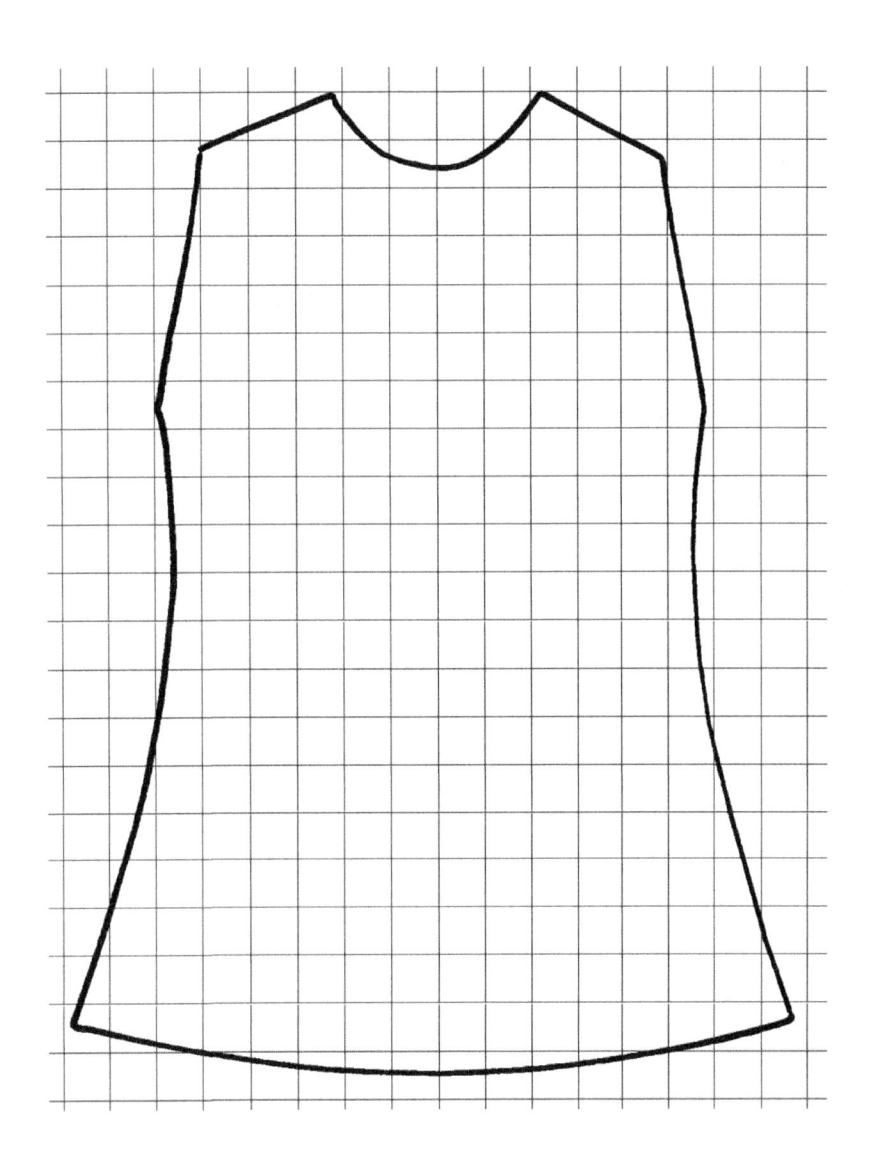

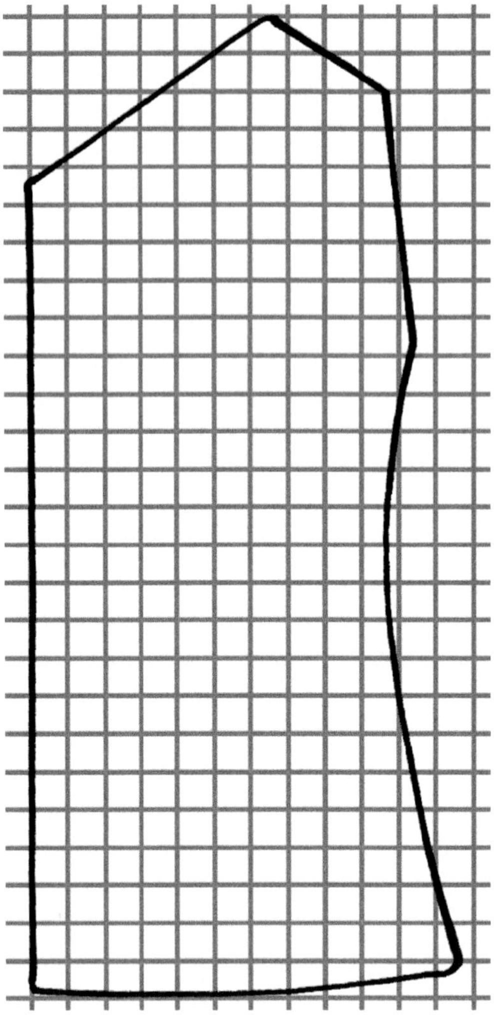

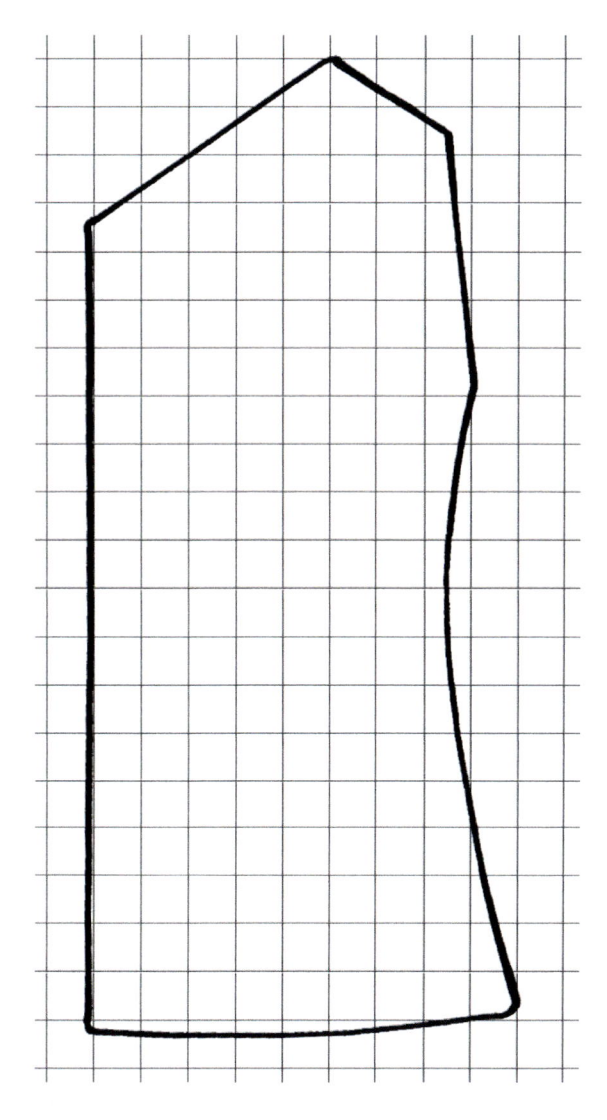

Cut them out and cut out another of the half pieces.

If you are using the paper book, cut out the three Dress pieces.

You should have 3 pieces.

If using squared paper then label each piece.

Lay each pattern piece on to your cotton fabric and draw around them.

Carefully cut them out.

Starting with the Front dress piece, fold over and sew a small hem along the bottom of the piece.

Do the same with the arms and neck.

Take the two back pieces and hem the bottom edges, sleeves and necklines.

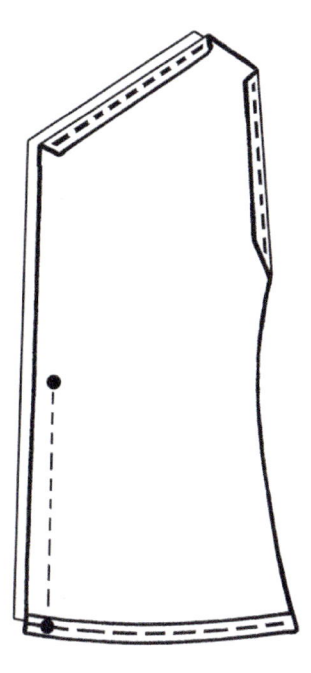

Place one back piece on top of the other and sew them together just half way up starting at the bottom edge.

Open out the two pieces.

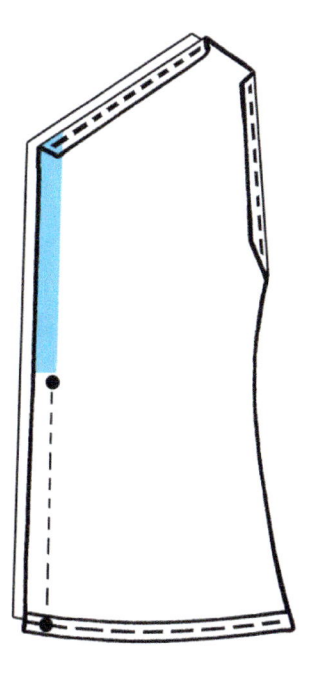

Fold over just one of the other halves of that side and sew it in position.

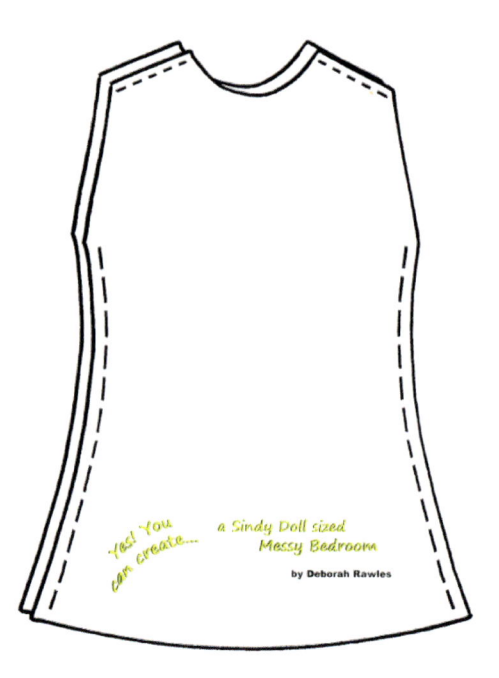

Lay the back piece on to the front piece, so that the inside of the fabric is facing you, and sew together the sides and shoulders.

Turn the dress in the right way and iron it.

Add a popper or snap fastening to the middle top corners at the back of the dress to complete it.

T-shirts

These are made in a similar way as the Dress you have just finished but are slightly easier.

You will need:

- Paper Pattern or 5mm squared paper (or Quad paper) and a Pencil
- Cotton T-shirting Fabric (make sure this is colour safe). An old T-shirt that has been washed many times would be perfect.
- Matching sewing thread
- Needle
- Scissors
- Hammer Popper or Hammer Snap Fastener
- Hammer
- Ballpoint pen or fabric pen

Method:

If you have not bought the paper copy of this book then you will need to create your own paper pattern pieces.

Begin by copying the lines, square by square on to your own Squared paper.

Choose the smaller squared pieces if you are using the 5mm Squared Paper and the larger squares for Quad paper.

Squared Paper
Front Piece

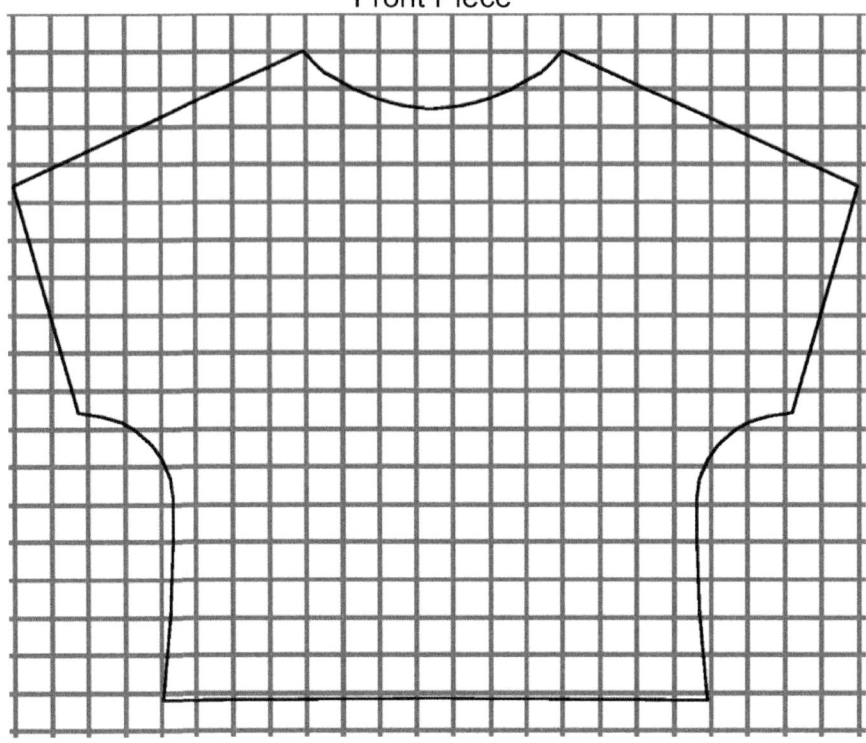

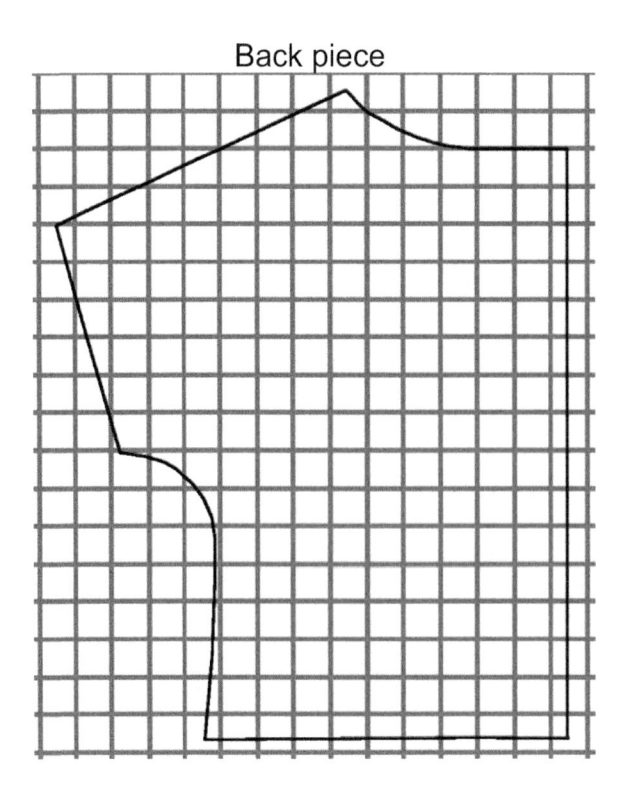

Back piece

Quad Paper
Front Piece

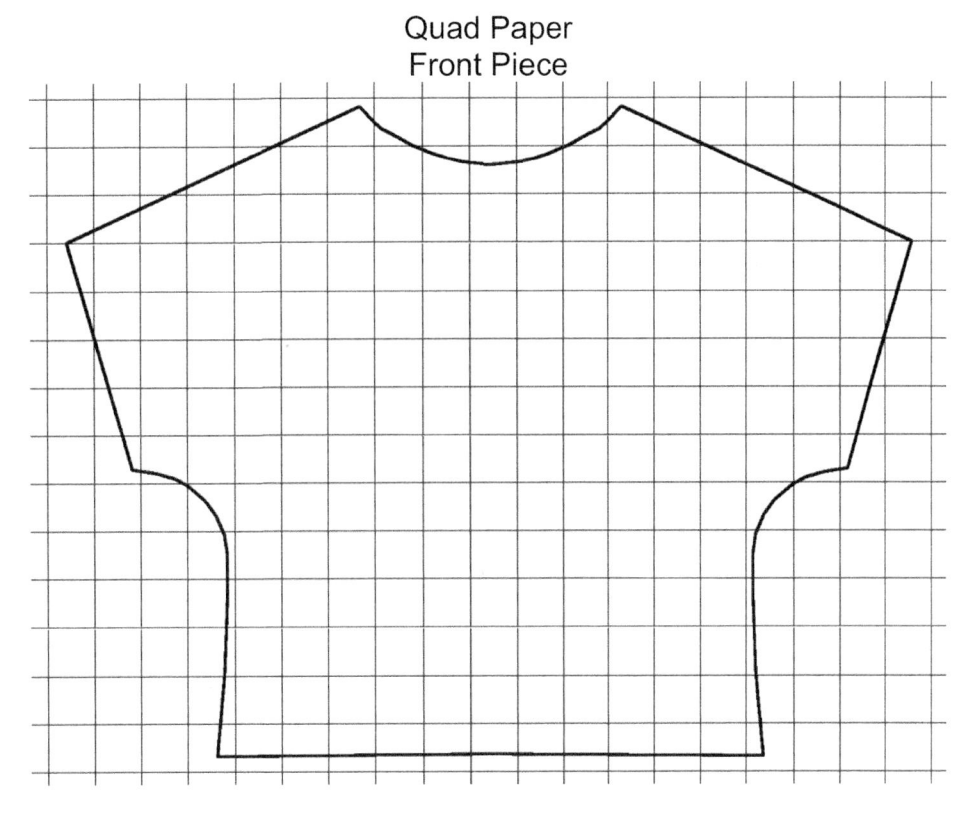

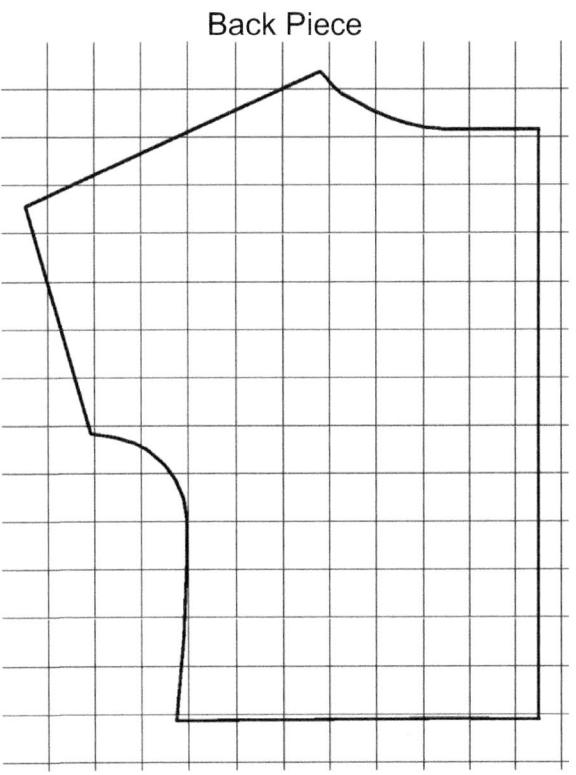

Back Piece

Cut them out and cut 2 of the back pieces.

Reverse one of the back pieces.

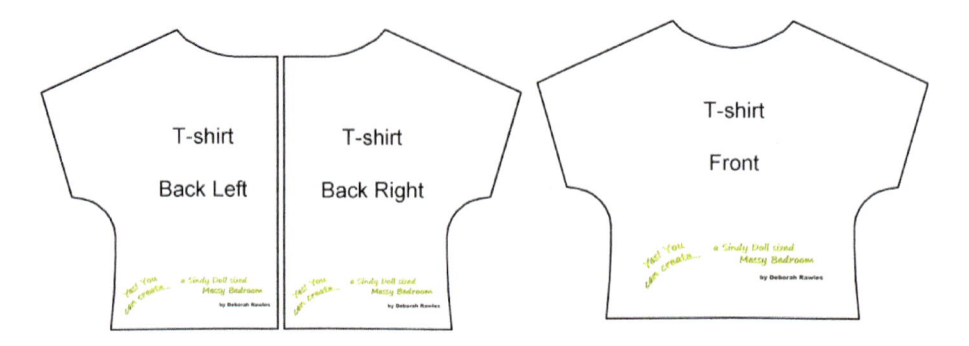

You should now have three pattern pieces.

Draw around each piece on to your cotton T-shirting fabric and cut them out.

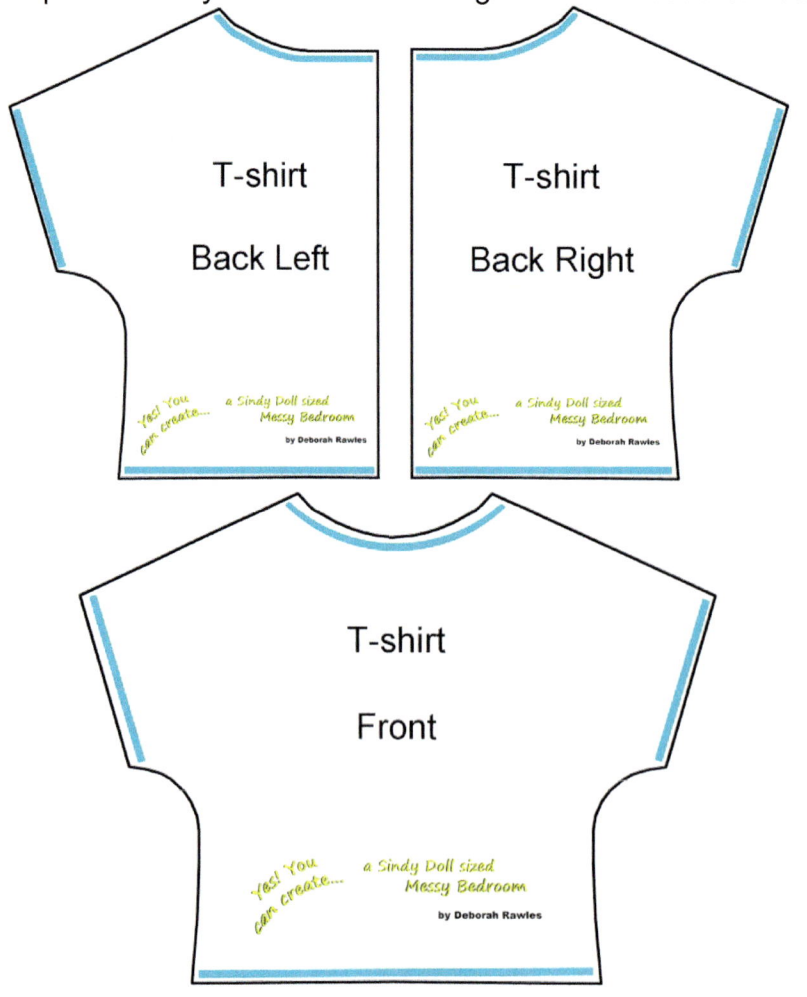

Hem the sleeves, collar and bottom of each piece.

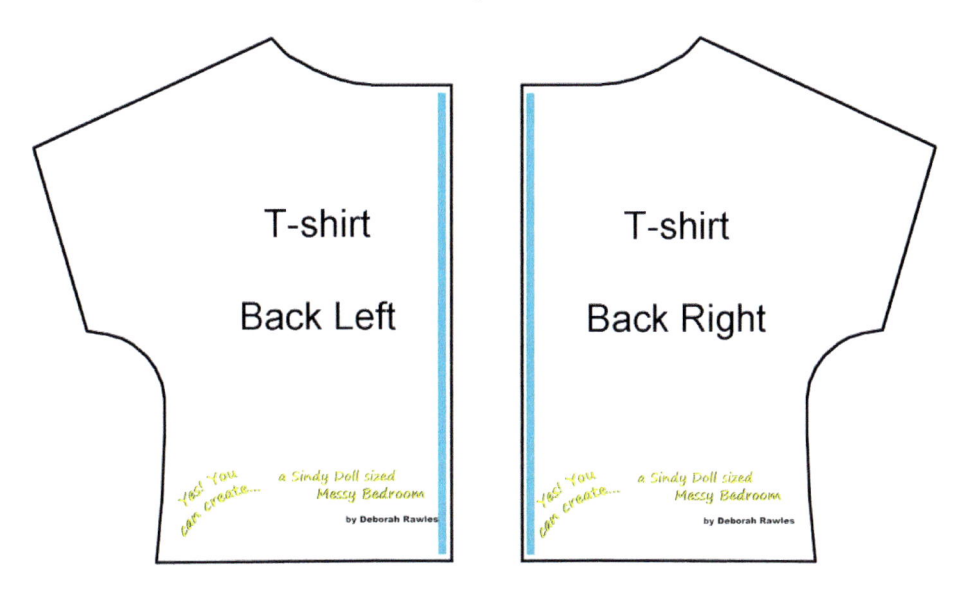

Then hem the long straight back seems on the back pieces.

Overlap these two pieces and lay them on top of the front piece (so the t-shirt is inside out).

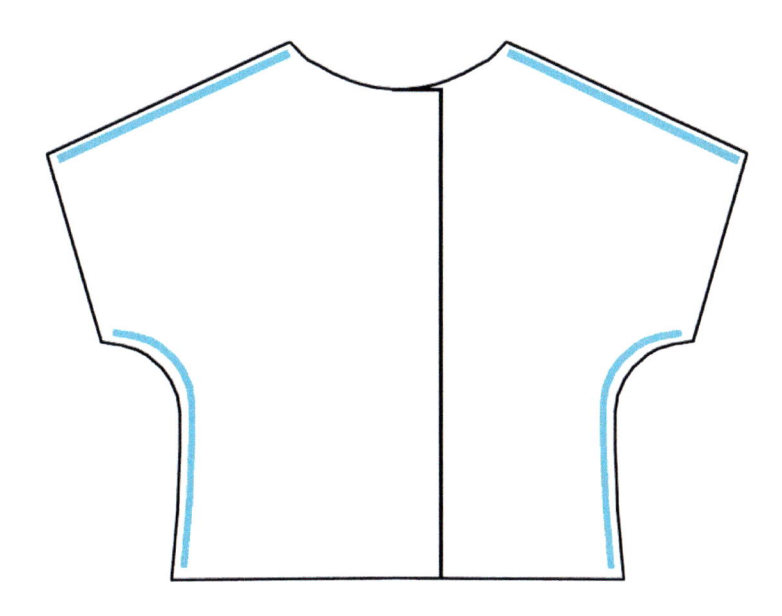

Sew together the shoulders and sides.

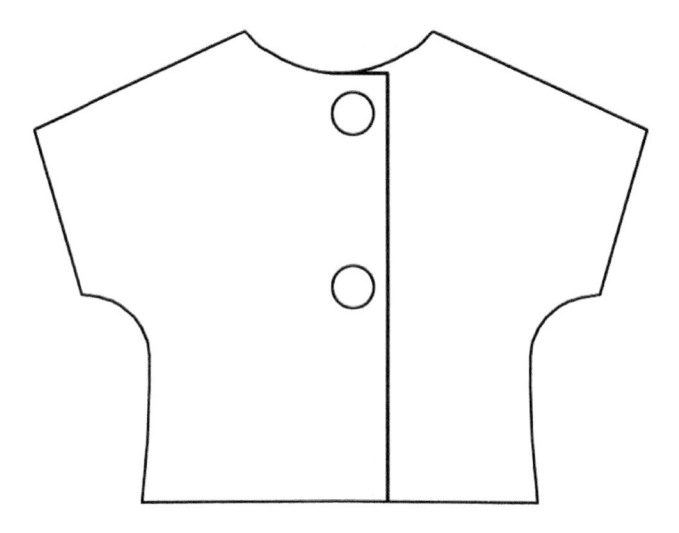

Add two poppers or snap fasteners at the back to complete your T-shirt.

Short socks

You will need:

- White Cotton T-shirting fabric
- White sewing thread
- A needle
- Scissors
- A Pencil
- Paper
- 5mm Squared or Quad Paper

Method:

If you are using the book then simply trace this template.

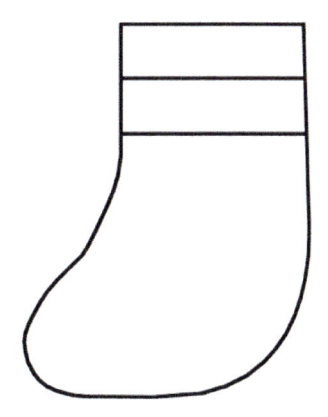

If not, then copy each square on to your squared paper.

5mm Squared Paper

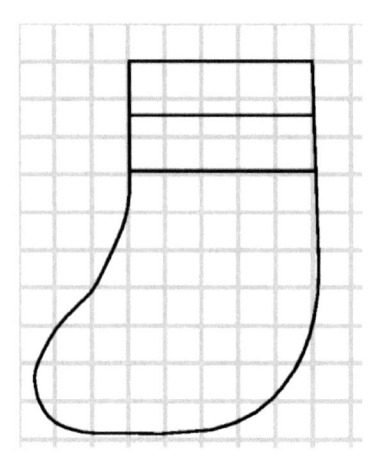

Quad Paper

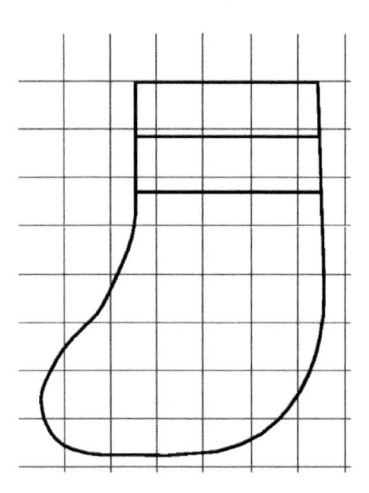

Cut out your template.

Cut a piece of White Cotton T-shirting measuring 10cm (4 inches) x 10cm (4 inches).

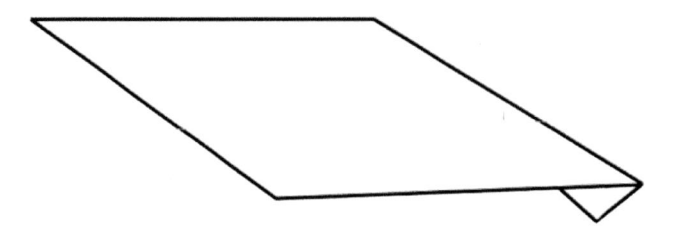

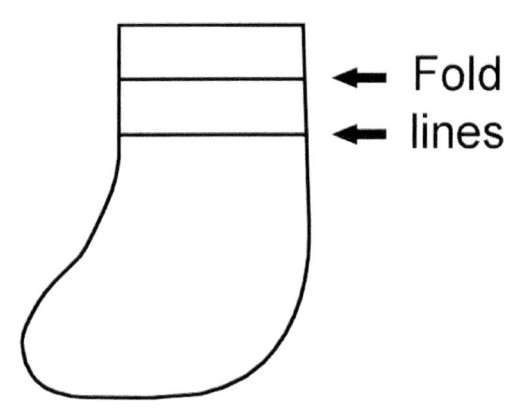

Fold over the top edge using the lines on the template as a guide to the width.

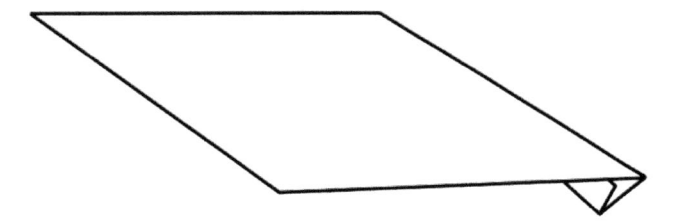

Fold it over again and carefully iron them flat.

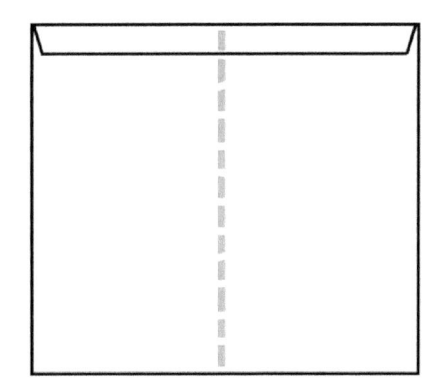

Fold the whole piece in half so that the folded edge is now sandwiched.

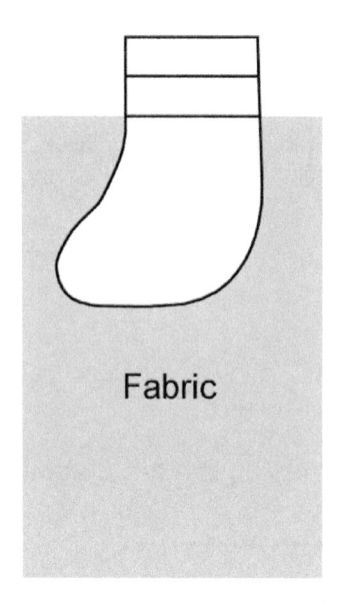

Place the sock template as shown (the folds are under the top edge) and draw around the bottom half of the template.

Sew along this line, making sure that the stitches go all the way through all the layers of fabric.

Cut around your stitching, not too close, and turn it in the right way out to complete your first sock.

Dream Catcher

You will need:

- Wire
- Wire cutters
- Thread
- Beads
- Sequins (Spangles) or feathers
- Scissors

Method:

Bend your Wire into a circle measuring about 6cm (2 ¼ inches) across. It does not need to be neat. Do a couple of loops and wind it around to make it look more handmade. This will be your frame.

Tie the end of a long piece of thread to the frame.

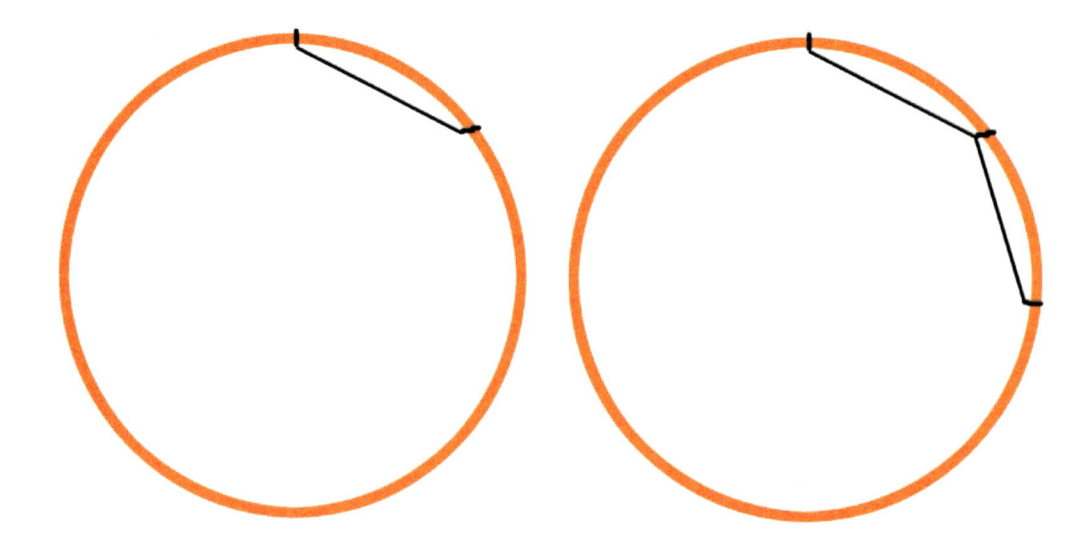

Tie it again at about 2.5cm (1 inch).

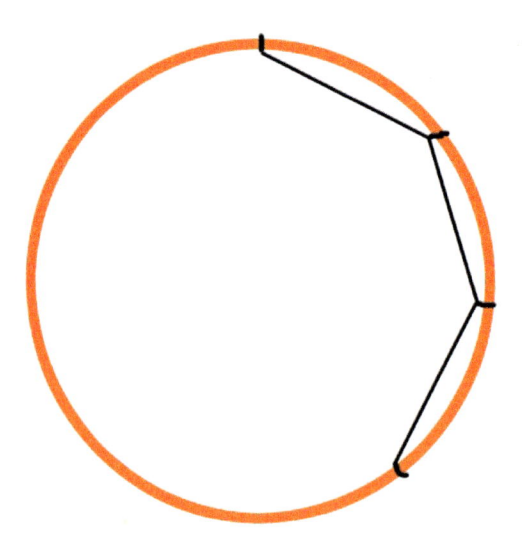

Continue to tie it at intervals, to the frame, until you get back to the beginning.

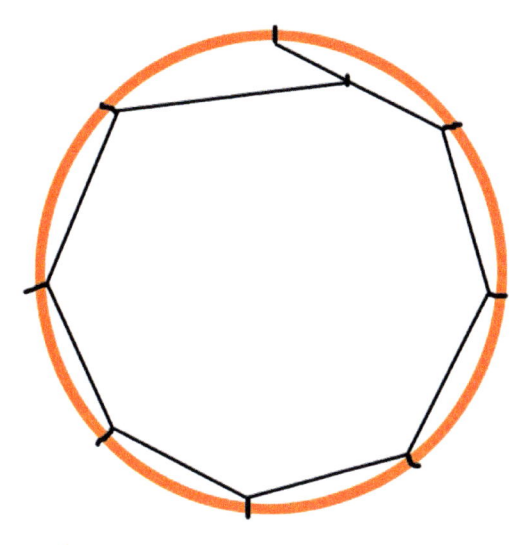

Next, instead of tying it to the frame, you tie it to the new thread circle you just created.

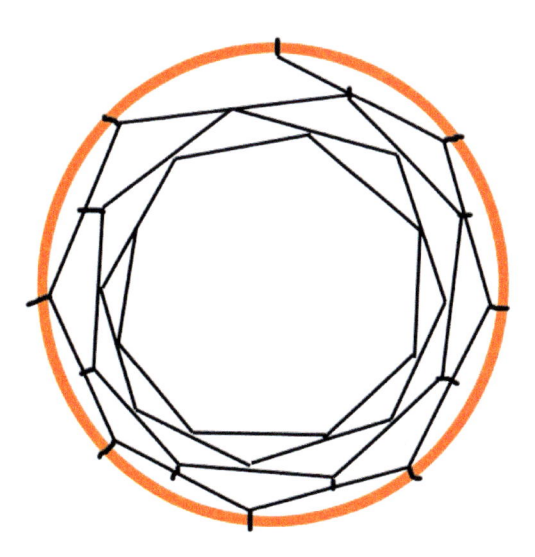

Continue to tie off in a spiral until you get to the centre, then knot it and cut off the extra thread.

Tie a feather or a sequin to the end of a separate piece of thread and thread some beads on to it.

Tie this to the bottom of the dream catcher.

Make 2 more and tie them either side.

Tie a hanging loop to the top to complete your dream catcher. These make lovely gifts for friends and family.

Waste Paper Bin

You can make a waste paper bin from many things like old bottle lids or the sauce holders from fast food restaurants,
but it is nice to make one that matches your dolls room.

You will need:

- Paper or thin card
- Scissors
- Pencil
- Glue
- 5mm squared paper or quad paper

Method:

Copy the template square by square on to your 5mm Squared paper or Quad paper.

Or use the template at the back of this book, if you have bought a printed copy.

5mm Squared Paper

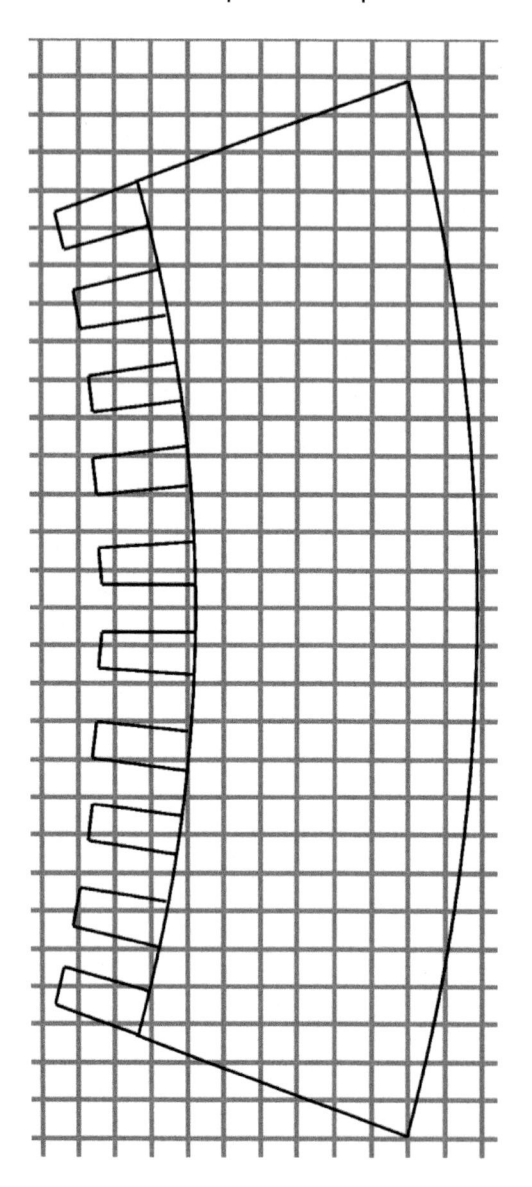

Quad Paper

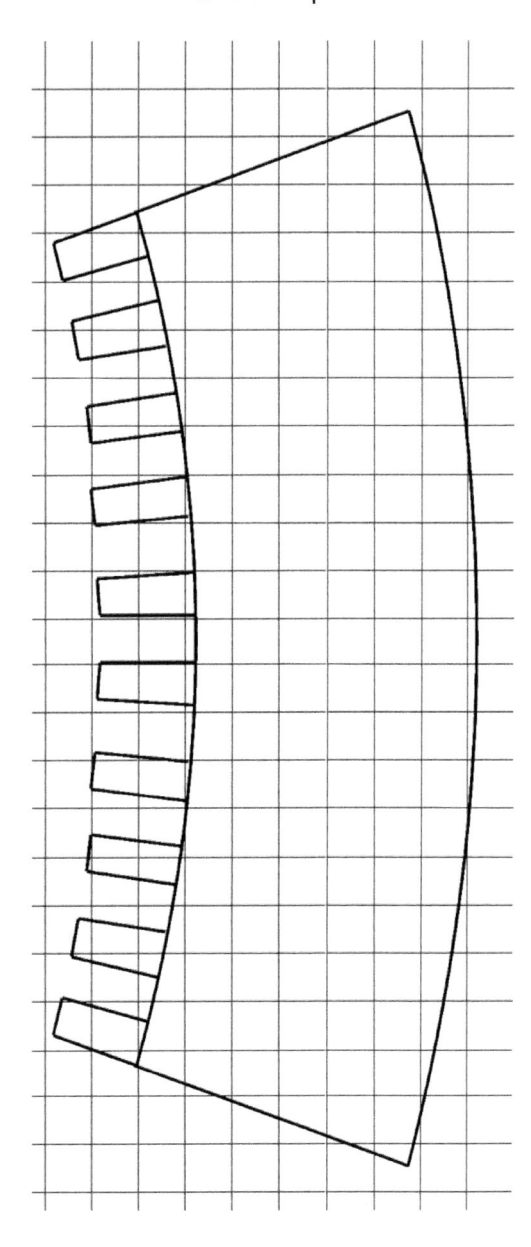

Draw around the template on to your chosen paper or card.

Cut it out.

Fold the flaps over.

Curve the whole piece over and glue one side to the other to create a cone with a hole at each end. One end will be larger than the other.

Place the narrowest end on to your chosen paper and draw around it.

Cut this circle out.

Put some glue on the tabs and glue it to the circle to create the base.

Scrunch up some old bits of tissue, or whatever small scraps you may have, and place them in your bin to complete it.

To make the lamp, simply cut another arch shaped piece but this time without the flaps. Glue it together to create a cone. Cut a strip of paper and glue it across the inside. You can use anything you like for the base, like an old jewellery box, bottle lid or even a painted stone! Glue the cone shade onto your chosen base to complete it.

Felt Shoulder Bag

With the range of colours of Felt available and embellishments, the range of bags you could create are endless. They are lovely to make to match your dolls outfit.

You will need:

- Coloured Felt
- Scissors
- Ruler
- Glue
- Sewing thread
- Needle

Method:

Cut 2 pieces of Felt measuring 2.7cm (1 inch) by 3.7cm (1 ½ inch).

Cut a long strip of Felt measuring 17cm (7 inches) by 7mm (1/4 inch).

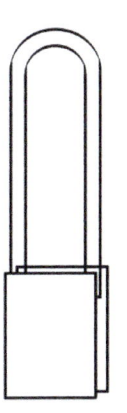

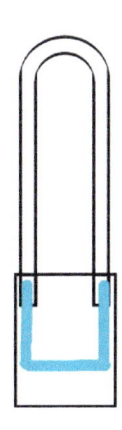

Sandwich the two ends between the 2 pieces and glue or sew them in place, running the glue two thirds of the way down the inside, across to the other side and back up to the top.

Allow the glue to dry.

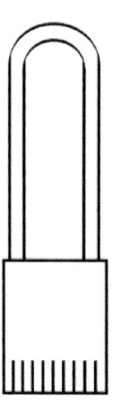

Make small cuts up from the bottom of the bag to the sew line or glue to create a fringe.

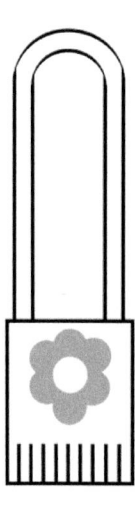

You can cut whatever shapes you like from different colour felt or fabrics to decorate your bag. You can use sequins or beads. Just glue them on to finish your own unique designed bag.

Chain Strap Shoulder Bag

You will need:

- Felt fabric
- Glue
- Chain
- Pliers
- Scissors
- 2 6mm Bolt rings

Method:

Cut a piece of Felt measuring 7.5cm (3 inches) by 4.5cm (1 ¾ inches).

Round off the corners at one end.

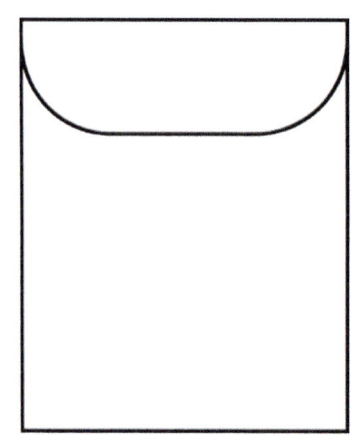

Fold the rounded end over by 1.5cm (1/4 inch) and use a small amount of glue to hold it down.

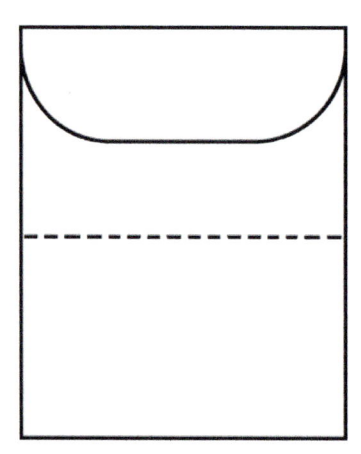

Fold up the other end so it goes under this flap and glue up each side to hold it. You may need to put the bag under a book or peg it while it dries.

Make a 18cm (7 inch) length of chain by opening a link with pliers.

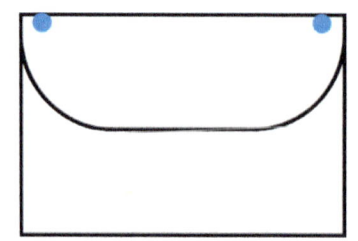

Open the chain at one end and clamp it shut with the top of the bag between it (or you can sew it in position). Do the same with the other end.

Using a little more chain open a link and clamp it around a 6mm Bolt ring.

Leave 3 links and clamp the other end to the other ring and stitch or glue it to the front of the bag.

You can use anything you have to decorate the front of the bag, broken earrings, beads etc.

Again, by changing the colour of the Felt fabric and decorations on the front of the bag you can have a huge variety of designs.

Beaded Bag

You will need:

- Leatherette Fabric (An old diary or notebook works well)
- Sewing Thread
- Needle
- Scissors
- Seed Beads

Cut a piece of Leatherette Fabric measuring 4.5cm (1 ¾ inch) by 2.8cm (1 1/8 inch).

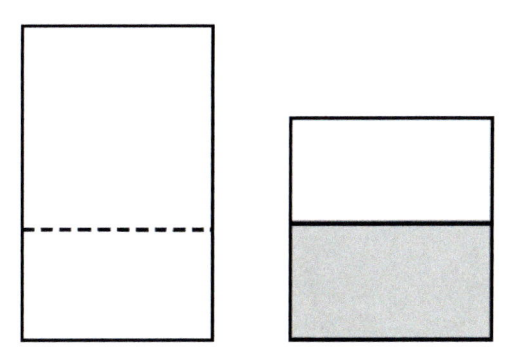

Fold the bottom over by 1.6cm (5/8 inch).

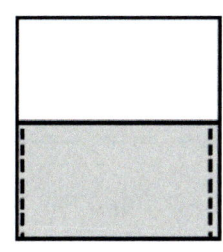

Sew it in place with a line of stitching at each side.

Take a piece of sewing thread and tie a big knot in the end.

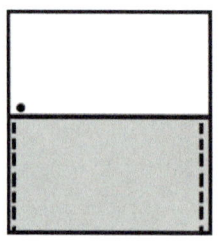

Sew it through the bag to make the start of the strap.

Thread enough Seed Beads on to it until it measures 12cm (4 ¾ inches).

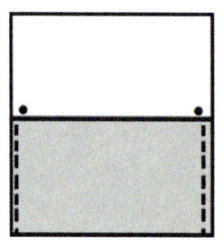

Sew it through the bag again, knot it well and cut off the extra thread.

Add some glue to the knots to ensure it does not come off.

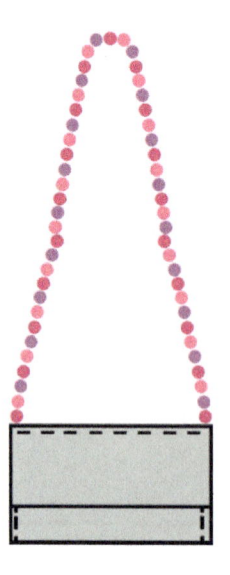

Fold over the flap and sew it in place to complete your Beaded Bag.

I hope you have enjoyed creating these makes for your dolls.

Wishing you many years of peaceful crafting.

Deborah Rawles

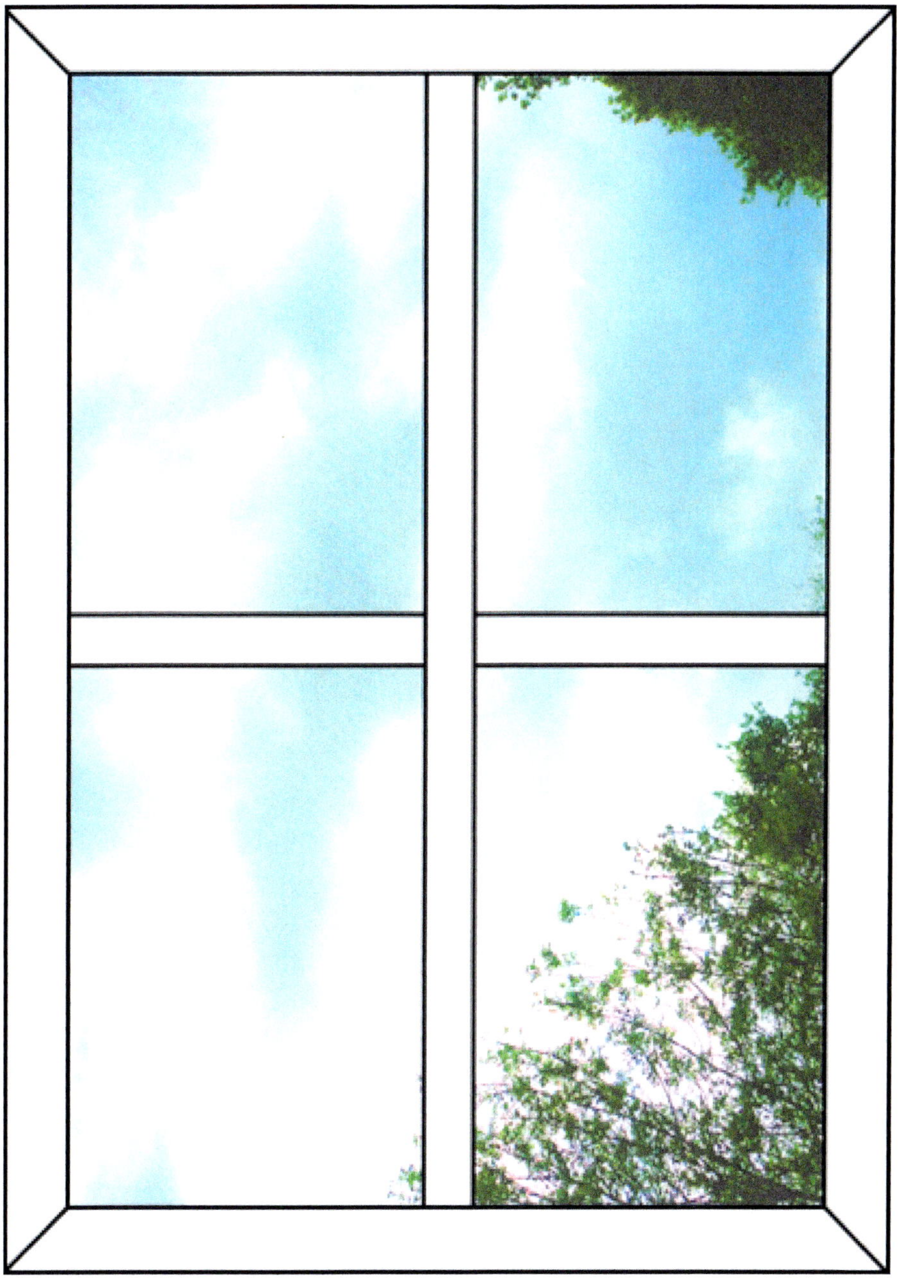

Hatbox Lid

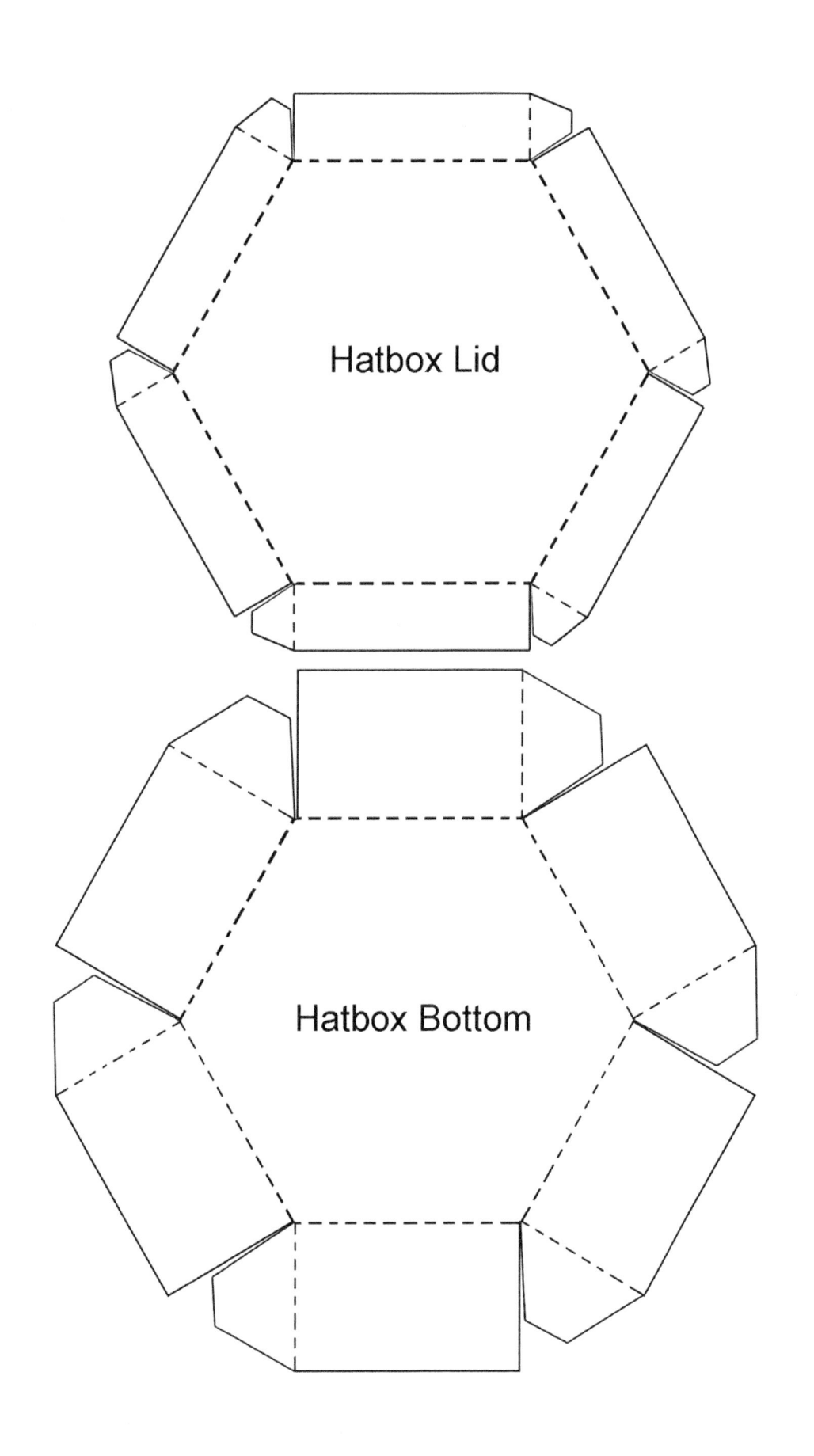

Hatbox Bottom

Doll Dress
Front

Yes! You can create.... *a Sindy Doll sized Messy Bedroom*

by Deborah Rawles

Doll Dress

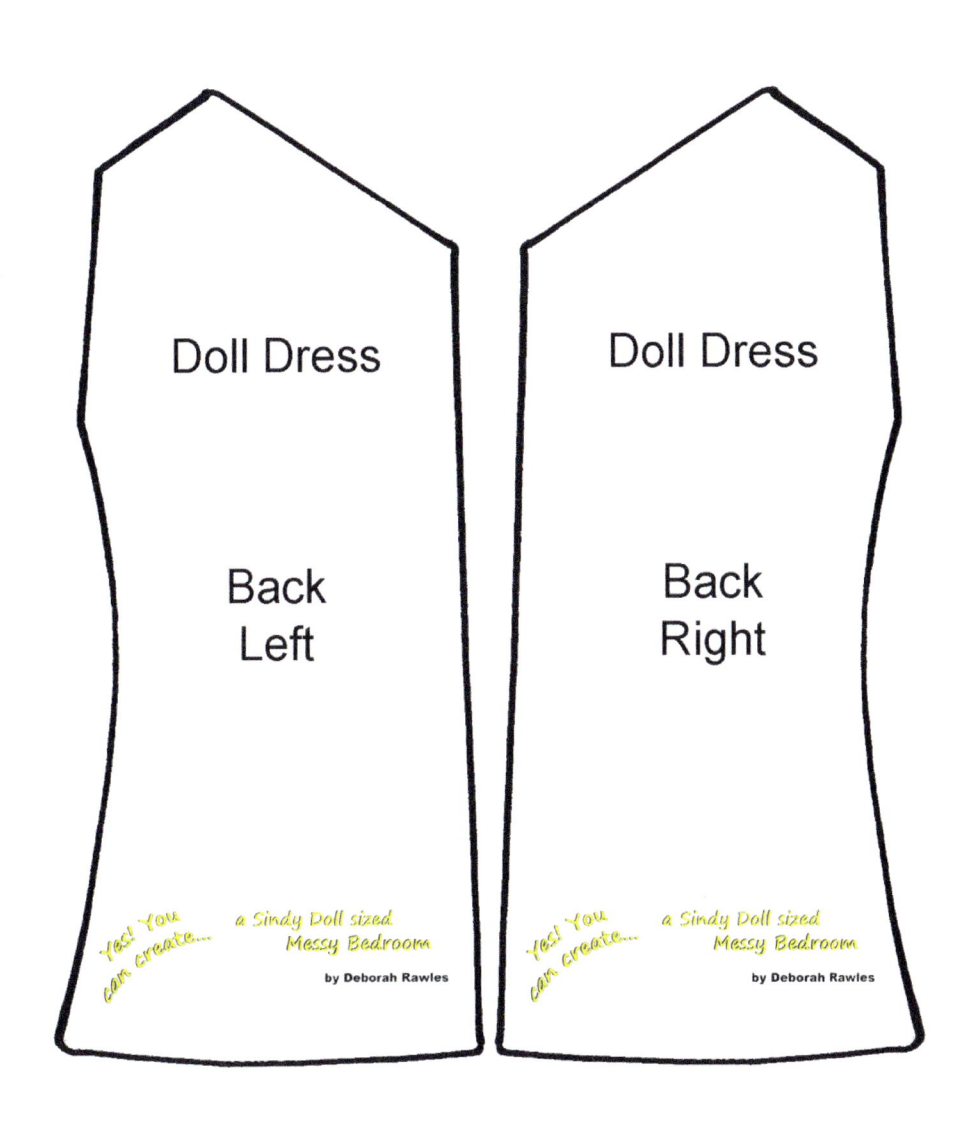

Back
Left

Yes! You can create....
a Sindy Doll sized
Messy Bedroom
by Deborah Rawles

Doll Dress

Back
Right

Yes! You can create....
a Sindy Doll sized
Messy Bedroom
by Deborah Rawles

T-shirt

Front

Yes! You can create.... *a Sindy Doll sized Messy Bedroom*

by Deborah Rawles

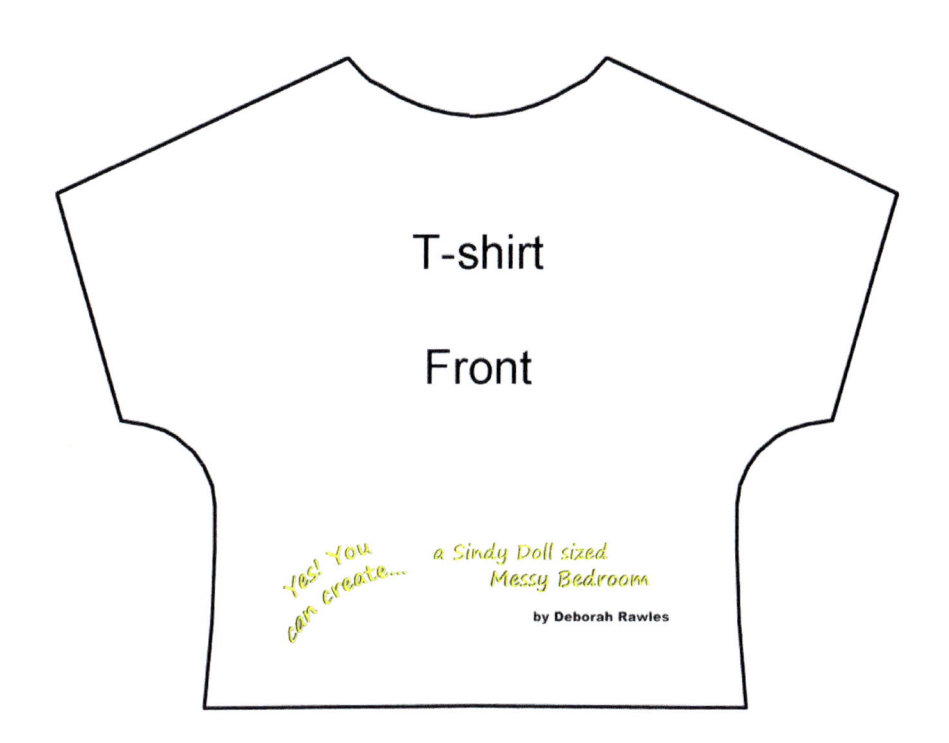

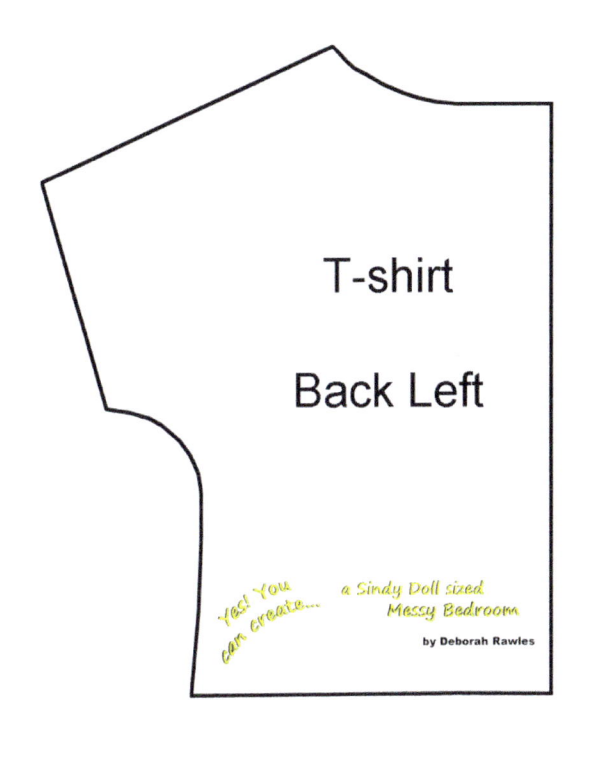

T-shirt

Back Left

Yes! You can create.... a Sindy Doll sized Messy Bedroom

by Deborah Rawles

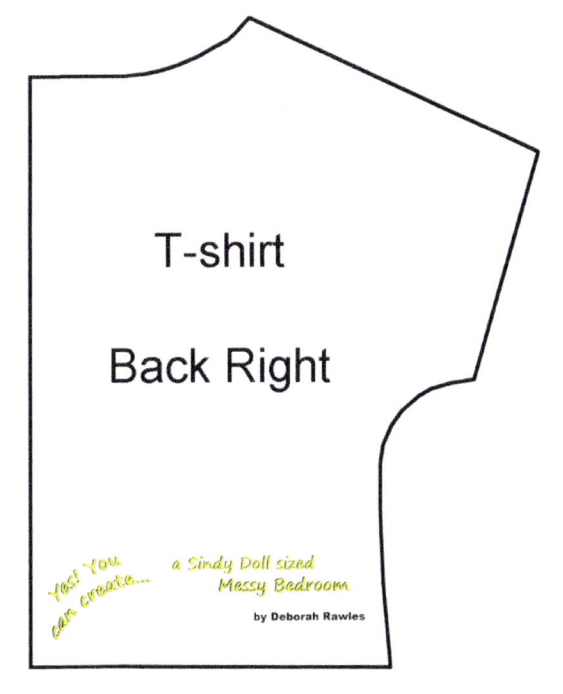

T-shirt

Back Right

Yes! You can create.... a Sindy Doll sized Messy Bedroom

by Deborah Rawles

Sock Template

Yes! You can create..... a Sindy Doll sized Messy Bedroom

by Deborah Rawles

WASTE PAPER BIN

Yes! You can create.... *a Sindy Doll sized Messy Bedroom*

by Deborah Rawles

1	2	3	4	5	6	7
8	9	10	11	12	13	14
15	16	17	18	19	20	21
22	23	24	25	26	27	28
29	30	31				

Other books by Deborah Rawles

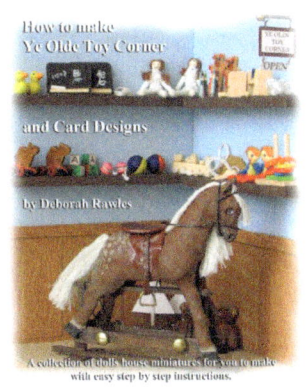

1 How to make Ye Olde Toy Corner and Card Designs

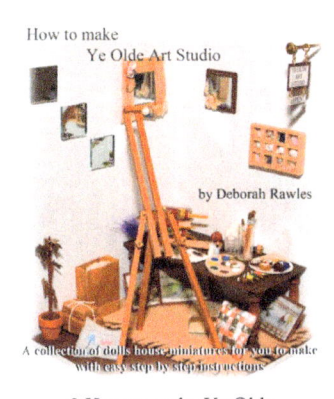

2 How to make Ye Olde Art Studio

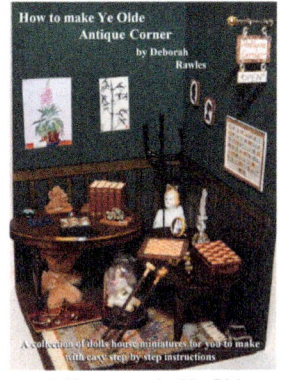

3 How to make Ye Olde Antiques Corner

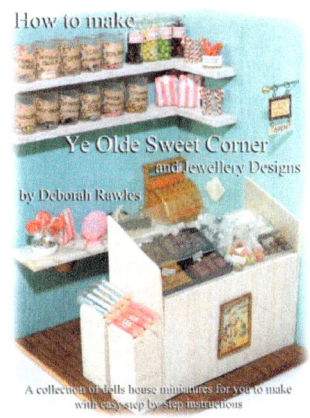

4 How to make Ye Olde Sweet Corner and Jewellery Designs

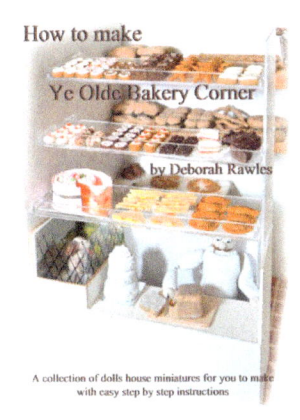

5 How to make Ye Olde Bakery Corner

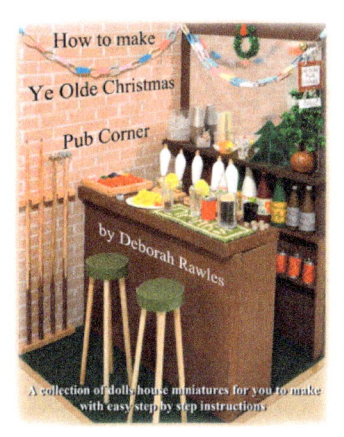

6 How to make Ye Olde Christmas Pub Corner

7 How to make Ye Olde Chocolate Corner

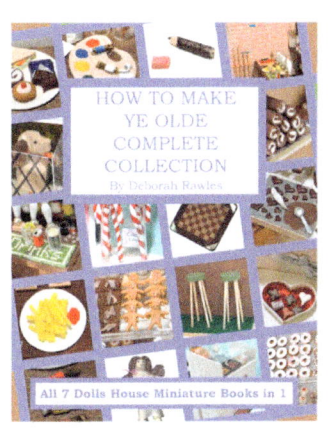

How to make Ye Olde Complete Collection

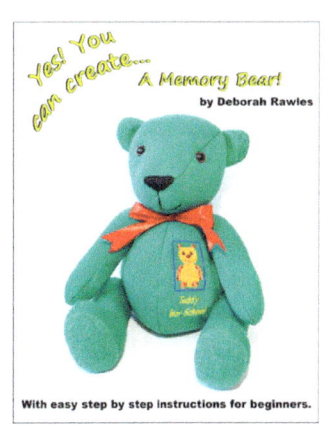

Printed in Great Britain
by Amazon